C-666 CAREER EXAMINATION SERIES

This is your
PASSBOOK for...

Real Estate Broker

Test Preparation Study Guide
Questions & Answers

NATIONAL LEARNING CORPORATION®

COPYRIGHT NOTICE

This book is SOLELY intended for, is sold ONLY to, and its use is RESTRICTED to individual, bona fide applicants or candidates who qualify by virtue of having seriously filed applications for appropriate license, certificate, professional and/or promotional advancement, higher school matriculation, scholarship, or other legitimate requirements of education and/or governmental authorities.

This book is NOT intended for use, class instruction, tutoring, training, duplication, copying, reprinting, excerption, or adaptation, etc., by:

1) Other publishers
2) Proprietors and/or Instructors of "Coaching" and/or Preparatory Courses
3) Personnel and/or Training Divisions of commercial, industrial, and governmental organizations
4) Schools, colleges, or universities and/or their departments and staffs, including teachers and other personnel
5) Testing Agencies or Bureaus
6) Study groups which seek by the purchase of a single volume to copy and/or duplicate and/or adapt this material for use by the group as a whole without having purchased individual volumes for each of the members of the group
7) Et al.

Such persons would be in violation of appropriate Federal and State statutes.

PROVISION OF LICENSING AGREEMENTS – Recognized educational, commercial, industrial, and governmental institutions and organizations, and others legitimately engaged in educational pursuits, including training, testing, and measurement activities, may address request for a licensing agreement to the copyright owners, who will determine whether, and under what conditions, including fees and charges, the materials in this book may be used them. In other words, a licensing facility exists for the legitimate use of the material in this book on other than an individual basis. However, it is asseverated and affirmed here that the material in this book CANNOT be used without the receipt of the express permission of such a licensing agreement from the Publishers. Inquiries re licensing should be addressed to the company, attention rights and permissions department.

All rights reserved, including the right of reproduction in whole or in part, in any form or by any means, electronic or mechanical, including photocopying, recording, or by any information storage and retrieval system, without permission in writing from the Publisher.

Copyright © 2025 by
National Learning Corporation

212 Michael Drive, Syosset, NY 11791
(516) 921-8888 • www.passbooks.com
E-mail: info@passbooks.com

PASSBOOK® SERIES

THE *PASSBOOK® SERIES* has been created to prepare applicants and candidates for the ultimate academic battlefield – the examination room.

At some time in our lives, each and every one of us may be required to take an examination – for validation, matriculation, admission, qualification, registration, certification, or licensure.

Based on the assumption that every applicant or candidate has met the basic formal educational standards, has taken the required number of courses, and read the necessary texts, the *PASSBOOK® SERIES* furnishes the one special preparation which may assure passing with confidence, instead of failing with insecurity. Examination questions – together with answers – are furnished as the basic vehicle for study so that the mysteries of the examination and its compounding difficulties may be eliminated or diminished by a sure method.

This book is meant to help you pass your examination provided that you qualify and are serious in your objective.

The entire field is reviewed through the huge store of content information which is succinctly presented through a provocative and challenging approach – the question-and-answer method.

A climate of success is established by furnishing the correct answers at the end of each test.

You soon learn to recognize types of questions, forms of questions, and patterns of questioning. You may even begin to anticipate expected outcomes.

You perceive that many questions are repeated or adapted so that you can gain acute insights, which may enable you to score many sure points.

You learn how to confront new questions, or types of questions, and to attack them confidently and work out the correct answers.

You note objectives and emphases, and recognize pitfalls and dangers, so that you may make positive educational adjustments.

Moreover, you are kept fully informed in relation to new concepts, methods, practices, and directions in the field.

You discover that you are actually taking the examination all the time: you are preparing for the examination by "taking" an examination, not by reading extraneous and/or supererogatory textbooks.

In short, this PASSBOOK®, used directedly, should be an important factor in helping you to pass your test.

REAL ESTATE BROKER

JOB DESCRIPTION

Real estate brokers are very similar to real estate agents, except brokers have met the licensing requirements necessary to manage their own real estate businesses. Real estate agents who haven't earned a broker license have to work with a broker.

Real estate brokers help their clients buy and sell residential and commercial properties. Some brokers specialize in selling one type of property, while others sell all types.

Real estate brokers often employ real estate agents to work for them. In these situations, brokers handle the business details required to get a property listed and paid for, and then they pay the agents a commission for each property that they sell. Property owners use real estate brokers because brokers have many marketing tools they can use to give their properties much more exposure than they would be able to get on their own. And because they know their local real estate market so well, brokers are able to offer advice on pricing and other factors that can impact the successful sale of a property. Property buyers use real estate brokers to help them find properties that meet their needs at the lowest price possible. In cases where a broker represents both the seller and the buyer, they have to disclose that fact to both sides. Regardless of whether they're working with a buyer or a seller, the goal of a real estate broker is to help their clients get the best deal that they can on their properties.

WORK ENVIRONMENT AND SCHEDULE

Most real estate brokers work in an office environment, but may spend a lot of their time traveling to meet with clients, view new properties for sale, and meet with potential clients. It's very common for real estate brokers to work more than forty hours per week. Because many of their clients work during regular business hours, it's often necessary for brokers to work on nights and weekends to accommodate their schedules.

Many brokers are able to set their own schedules, which many people consider to be one of the most appealing aspects of this occupation.

HOW TO TAKE A TEST

I. YOU MUST PASS AN EXAMINATION

A. WHAT EVERY CANDIDATE SHOULD KNOW

Examination applicants often ask us for help in preparing for the written test. What can I study in advance? What kinds of questions will be asked? How will the test be given? How will the papers be graded?

As an applicant for a civil service examination, you may be wondering about some of these things. Our purpose here is to suggest effective methods of advance study and to describe civil service examinations.

Your chances for success on this examination can be increased if you know how to prepare. Those "pre-examination jitters" can be reduced if you know what to expect. You can even experience an adventure in good citizenship if you know why civil service exams are given.

B. WHY ARE CIVIL SERVICE EXAMINATIONS GIVEN?

Civil service examinations are important to you in two ways. As a citizen, you want public jobs filled by employees who know how to do their work. As a job seeker, you want a fair chance to compete for that job on an equal footing with other candidates. The best-known means of accomplishing this two-fold goal is the competitive examination.

Exams are widely publicized throughout the nation. They may be administered for jobs in federal, state, city, municipal, town or village governments or agencies.

Any citizen may apply, with some limitations, such as the age or residence of applicants. Your experience and education may be reviewed to see whether you meet the requirements for the particular examination. When these requirements exist, they are reasonable and applied consistently to all applicants. Thus, a competitive examination may cause you some uneasiness now, but it is your privilege and safeguard.

C. HOW ARE CIVIL SERVICE EXAMS DEVELOPED?

Examinations are carefully written by trained technicians who are specialists in the field known as "psychological measurement," in consultation with recognized authorities in the field of work that the test will cover. These experts recommend the subject matter areas or skills to be tested; only those knowledges or skills important to your success on the job are included. The most reliable books and source materials available are used as references. Together, the experts and technicians judge the difficulty level of the questions.

Test technicians know how to phrase questions so that the problem is clearly stated. Their ethics do not permit "trick" or "catch" questions. Questions may have been tried out on sample groups, or subjected to statistical analysis, to determine their usefulness.

Written tests are often used in combination with performance tests, ratings of training and experience, and oral interviews. All of these measures combine to form the best-known means of finding the right person for the right job.

II. HOW TO PASS THE WRITTEN TEST

A. NATURE OF THE EXAMINATION

To prepare intelligently for civil service examinations, you should know how they differ from school examinations you have taken. In school you were assigned certain definite pages to read or subjects to cover. The examination questions were quite detailed and usually emphasized memory. Civil service exams, on the other hand, try to discover your present ability to perform the duties of a position, plus your potentiality to learn these duties. In other words, a civil service exam attempts to predict how successful you will be. Questions cover such a broad area that they cannot be as minute and detailed as school exam questions.

In the public service similar kinds of work, or positions, are grouped together in one "class." This process is known as *position-classification*. All the positions in a class are paid according to the salary range for that class. One class title covers all of these positions, and they are all tested by the same examination.

B. FOUR BASIC STEPS

1) Study the announcement

How, then, can you know what subjects to study? Our best answer is: "Learn as much as possible about the class of positions for which you've applied." The exam will test the knowledge, skills and abilities needed to do the work.

Your most valuable source of information about the position you want is the official exam announcement. This announcement lists the training and experience qualifications. Check these standards and apply only if you come reasonably close to meeting them.

The brief description of the position in the examination announcement offers some clues to the subjects which will be tested. Think about the job itself. Review the duties in your mind. Can you perform them, or are there some in which you are rusty? Fill in the blank spots in your preparation.

Many jurisdictions preview the written test in the exam announcement by including a section called "Knowledge and Abilities Required," "Scope of the Examination," or some similar heading. Here you will find out specifically what fields will be tested.

2) Review your own background

Once you learn in general what the position is all about, and what you need to know to do the work, ask yourself which subjects you already know fairly well and which need improvement. You may wonder whether to concentrate on improving your strong areas or on building some background in your fields of weakness. When the announcement has specified "some knowledge" or "considerable knowledge," or has used adjectives like "beginning principles of..." or "advanced ... methods," you can get a clue as to the number and difficulty of questions to be asked in any given field. More questions, and hence broader coverage, would be included for those subjects which are more important in the work. Now weigh your strengths and weaknesses against the job requirements and prepare accordingly.

3) Determine the level of the position

Another way to tell how intensively you should prepare is to understand the level of the job for which you are applying. Is it the entering level? In other words, is this the position in which beginners in a field of work are hired? Or is it an intermediate or advanced level? Sometimes this is indicated by such words as "Junior" or "Senior" in the class title. Other jurisdictions use Roman numerals to designate the level – Clerk I, Clerk II, for example. The word "Supervisor" sometimes appears in the title. If the level is not indicated by the title, check the description of duties. Will you be working under very close supervision, or will you have responsibility for independent decisions in this work?

4) Choose appropriate study materials

Now that you know the subjects to be examined and the relative amount of each subject to be covered, you can choose suitable study materials. For beginning level jobs, or even advanced ones, if you have a pronounced weakness in some aspect of your training, read a modern, standard textbook in that field. Be sure it is up to date and has general coverage. Such books are normally available at your library, and the librarian will be glad to help you locate one. For entry-level positions, questions of appropriate difficulty are chosen – neither highly advanced questions, nor those too simple. Such questions require careful thought but not advanced training.

If the position for which you are applying is technical or advanced, you will read more advanced, specialized material. If you are already familiar with the basic principles of your field, elementary textbooks would waste your time. Concentrate on advanced textbooks and technical periodicals. Think through the concepts and review difficult problems in your field.

These are all general sources. You can get more ideas on your own initiative, following these leads. For example, training manuals and publications of the government agency which employs workers in your field can be useful, particularly for technical and professional positions. A letter or visit to the government department involved may result in more specific study suggestions, and certainly will provide you with a more definite idea of the exact nature of the position you are seeking.

III. KINDS OF TESTS

Tests are used for purposes other than measuring knowledge and ability to perform specified duties. For some positions, it is equally important to test ability to make adjustments to new situations or to profit from training. In others, basic mental abilities not dependent on information are essential. Questions which test these things may not appear as pertinent to the duties of the position as those which test for knowledge and information. Yet they are often highly important parts of a fair examination. For very general questions, it is almost impossible to help you direct your study efforts. What we can do is to point out some of the more common of these general abilities needed in public service positions and describe some typical questions.

1) General information

Broad, general information has been found useful for predicting job success in some kinds of work. This is tested in a variety of ways, from vocabulary lists to questions about current events. Basic background in some field of work, such as sociology or economics, may be sampled in a group of questions. Often these are principles which have become familiar to most persons through exposure rather than through formal training. It is difficult to advise you how to study for these questions; being alert to the world around you is our best suggestion.

2) Verbal ability

An example of an ability needed in many positions is verbal or language ability. Verbal ability is, in brief, the ability to use and understand words. Vocabulary and grammar tests are typical measures of this ability. Reading comprehension or paragraph interpretation questions are common in many kinds of civil service tests. You are given a paragraph of written material and asked to find its central meaning.

3) Numerical ability

Number skills can be tested by the familiar arithmetic problem, by checking paired lists of numbers to see which are alike and which are different, or by interpreting charts and graphs. In the latter test, a graph may be printed in the test booklet which you are asked to use as the basis for answering questions.

4) Observation

A popular test for law-enforcement positions is the observation test. A picture is shown to you for several minutes, then taken away. Questions about the picture test your ability to observe both details and larger elements.

5) Following directions

In many positions in the public service, the employee must be able to carry out written instructions dependably and accurately. You may be given a chart with several columns, each column listing a variety of information. The questions require you to carry out directions involving the information given in the chart.

6) Skills and aptitudes

Performance tests effectively measure some manual skills and aptitudes. When the skill is one in which you are trained, such as typing or shorthand, you can practice. These tests are often very much like those given in business school or high school courses. For many of the other skills and aptitudes, however, no short-time preparation can be made. Skills and abilities natural to you or that you have developed throughout your lifetime are being tested.

Many of the general questions just described provide all the data needed to answer the questions and ask you to use your reasoning ability to find the answers. Your best preparation for these tests, as well as for tests of facts and ideas, is to be at your physical and mental best. You, no doubt, have your own methods of getting into an exam-taking mood and keeping "in shape." The next section lists some ideas on this subject.

IV. KINDS OF QUESTIONS

Only rarely is the "essay" question, which you answer in narrative form, used in civil service tests. Civil service tests are usually of the short-answer type. Full instructions for answering these questions will be given to you at the examination. But in case this is your first experience with short-answer questions and separate answer sheets, here is what you need to know:

1) Multiple-choice Questions

Most popular of the short-answer questions is the "multiple choice" or "best answer" question. It can be used, for example, to test for factual knowledge, ability to solve problems or judgment in meeting situations found at work.

A multiple-choice question is normally one of three types—
- It can begin with an incomplete statement followed by several possible endings. You are to find the one ending which *best* completes the statement, although some of the others may not be entirely wrong.
- It can also be a complete statement in the form of a question which is answered by choosing one of the statements listed.

- It can be in the form of a problem – again you select the best answer.

Here is an example of a multiple-choice question with a discussion which should give you some clues as to the method for choosing the right answer:

When an employee has a complaint about his assignment, the action which will *best* help him overcome his difficulty is to
  A. discuss his difficulty with his coworkers
  B. take the problem to the head of the organization
  C. take the problem to the person who gave him the assignment
  D. say nothing to anyone about his complaint

In answering this question, you should study each of the choices to find which is best. Consider choice "A" – Certainly an employee may discuss his complaint with fellow employees, but no change or improvement can result, and the complaint remains unresolved. Choice "B" is a poor choice since the head of the organization probably does not know what assignment you have been given, and taking your problem to him is known as "going over the head" of the supervisor. The supervisor, or person who made the assignment, is the person who can clarify it or correct any injustice. Choice "C" is, therefore, correct. To say nothing, as in choice "D," is unwise. Supervisors have and interest in knowing the problems employees are facing, and the employee is seeking a solution to his problem.

2) True/False Questions

The "true/false" or "right/wrong" form of question is sometimes used. Here a complete statement is given. Your job is to decide whether the statement is right or wrong.

SAMPLE: A roaming cell-phone call to a nearby city costs less than a non-roaming call to a distant city.

This statement is wrong, or false, since roaming calls are more expensive.

This is not a complete list of all possible question forms, although most of the others are variations of these common types. You will always get complete directions for answering questions. Be sure you understand *how* to mark your answers – ask questions until you do.

V. RECORDING YOUR ANSWERS

Computer terminals are used more and more today for many different kinds of exams.
For an examination with very few applicants, you may be told to record your answers in the test booklet itself. Separate answer sheets are much more common. If this separate answer sheet is to be scored by machine – and this is often the case – it is highly important that you mark your answers correctly in order to get credit.
An electronic scoring machine is often used in civil service offices because of the speed with which papers can be scored. Machine-scored answer sheets must be marked with a pencil, which will be given to you. This pencil has a high graphite content which responds to the electronic scoring machine. As a matter of fact, stray dots may register as answers, so do not let your pencil rest on the answer sheet while you are pondering the correct answer. Also, if your pencil lead breaks or is otherwise defective, ask for another.

Since the answer sheet will be dropped in a slot in the scoring machine, be careful not to bend the corners or get the paper crumpled.

The answer sheet normally has five vertical columns of numbers, with 30 numbers to a column. These numbers correspond to the question numbers in your test booklet. After each number, going across the page are four or five pairs of dotted lines. These short dotted lines have small letters or numbers above them. The first two pairs may also have a "T" or "F" above the letters. This indicates that the first two pairs only are to be used if the questions are of the true-false type. If the questions are multiple choice, disregard the "T" and "F" and pay attention only to the small letters or numbers.

Answer your questions in the manner of the sample that follows:

32. The largest city in the United States is
   A. Washington, D.C.
   B. New York City
   C. Chicago
   D. Detroit
   E. San Francisco

1) Choose the answer you think is best. (New York City is the largest, so "B" is correct.)
2) Find the row of dotted lines numbered the same as the question you are answering. (Find row number 32)
3) Find the pair of dotted lines corresponding to the answer. (Find the pair of lines under the mark "B.")
4) Make a solid black mark between the dotted lines.

VI. BEFORE THE TEST

Common sense will help you find procedures to follow to get ready for an examination. Too many of us, however, overlook these sensible measures. Indeed, nervousness and fatigue have been found to be the most serious reasons why applicants fail to do their best on civil service tests. Here is a list of reminders:

- Begin your preparation early – Don't wait until the last minute to go scurrying around for books and materials or to find out what the position is all about.
- Prepare continuously – An hour a night for a week is better than an all-night cram session. This has been definitely established. What is more, a night a week for a month will return better dividends than crowding your study into a shorter period of time.
- Locate the place of the exam – You have been sent a notice telling you when and where to report for the examination. If the location is in a different town or otherwise unfamiliar to you, it would be well to inquire the best route and learn something about the building.
- Relax the night before the test – Allow your mind to rest. Do not study at all that night. Plan some mild recreation or diversion; then go to bed early and get a good night's sleep.
- Get up early enough to make a leisurely trip to the place for the test – This way unforeseen events, traffic snarls, unfamiliar buildings, etc. will not upset you.
- Dress comfortably – A written test is not a fashion show. You will be known by number and not by name, so wear something comfortable.

- Leave excess paraphernalia at home – Shopping bags and odd bundles will get in your way. You need bring only the items mentioned in the official notice you received; usually everything you need is provided. Do not bring reference books to the exam. They will only confuse those last minutes and be taken away from you when in the test room.
- Arrive somewhat ahead of time – If because of transportation schedules you must get there very early, bring a newspaper or magazine to take your mind off yourself while waiting.
- Locate the examination room – When you have found the proper room, you will be directed to the seat or part of the room where you will sit. Sometimes you are given a sheet of instructions to read while you are waiting. Do not fill out any forms until you are told to do so; just read them and be prepared.
- Relax and prepare to listen to the instructions
- If you have any physical problem that may keep you from doing your best, be sure to tell the test administrator. If you are sick or in poor health, you really cannot do your best on the exam. You can come back and take the test some other time.

VII. AT THE TEST

The day of the test is here and you have the test booklet in your hand. The temptation to get going is very strong. Caution! There is more to success than knowing the right answers. You must know how to identify your papers and understand variations in the type of short-answer question used in this particular examination. Follow these suggestions for maximum results from your efforts:

1) Cooperate with the monitor

The test administrator has a duty to create a situation in which you can be as much at ease as possible. He will give instructions, tell you when to begin, check to see that you are marking your answer sheet correctly, and so on. He is not there to guard you, although he will see that your competitors do not take unfair advantage. He wants to help you do your best.

2) Listen to all instructions

Don't jump the gun! Wait until you understand all directions. In most civil service tests you get more time than you need to answer the questions. So don't be in a hurry. Read each word of instructions until you clearly understand the meaning. Study the examples, listen to all announcements and follow directions. Ask questions if you do not understand what to do.

3) Identify your papers

Civil service exams are usually identified by number only. You will be assigned a number; you must not put your name on your test papers. Be sure to copy your number correctly. Since more than one exam may be given, copy your exact examination title.

4) Plan your time

Unless you are told that a test is a "speed" or "rate of work" test, speed itself is usually not important. Time enough to answer all the questions will be provided, but this does not mean that you have all day. An overall time limit has been set. Divide the total time (in minutes) by the number of questions to determine the approximate time you have for each question.

5) Do not linger over difficult questions

If you come across a difficult question, mark it with a paper clip (useful to have along) and come back to it when you have been through the booklet. One caution if you do this – be sure to skip a number on your answer sheet as well. Check often to be sure that you have not lost your place and that you are marking in the row numbered the same as the question you are answering.

6) Read the questions

Be sure you know what the question asks! Many capable people are unsuccessful because they failed to *read* the questions correctly.

7) Answer all questions

Unless you have been instructed that a penalty will be deducted for incorrect answers, it is better to guess than to omit a question.

8) Speed tests

It is often better NOT to guess on speed tests. It has been found that on timed tests people are tempted to spend the last few seconds before time is called in marking answers at random – without even reading them – in the hope of picking up a few extra points. To discourage this practice, the instructions may warn you that your score will be "corrected" for guessing. That is, a penalty will be applied. The incorrect answers will be deducted from the correct ones, or some other penalty formula will be used.

9) Review your answers

If you finish before time is called, go back to the questions you guessed or omitted to give them further thought. Review other answers if you have time.

10) Return your test materials

If you are ready to leave before others have finished or time is called, take ALL your materials to the monitor and leave quietly. Never take any test material with you. The monitor can discover whose papers are not complete, and taking a test booklet may be grounds for disqualification.

VIII. EXAMINATION TECHNIQUES

1) Read the general instructions carefully. These are usually printed on the first page of the exam booklet. As a rule, these instructions refer to the timing of the examination; the fact that you should not start work until the signal and must stop work at a signal, etc. If there are any *special* instructions, such as a choice of questions to be answered, make sure that you note this instruction carefully.

2) When you are ready to start work on the examination, that is as soon as the signal has been given, read the instructions to each question booklet, underline any key words or phrases, such as *least, best, outline, describe* and the like. In this way you will tend to answer as requested rather than discover on reviewing your paper that you *listed without describing*, that you selected the *worst* choice rather than the *best* choice, etc.

3) If the examination is of the objective or multiple-choice type – that is, each question will also give a series of possible answers: A, B, C or D, and you are called upon to select the best answer and write the letter next to that answer on your answer paper – it is advisable to start answering each question in turn. There may be anywhere from 50 to 100 such questions in the three or four hours allotted and you can see how much time would be taken if you read through all the questions before beginning to answer any. Furthermore, if you come across a question or group of questions which you know would be difficult to answer, it would undoubtedly affect your handling of all the other questions.

4) If the examination is of the essay type and contains but a few questions, it is a moot point as to whether you should read all the questions before starting to answer any one. Of course, if you are given a choice – say five out of seven and the like – then it is essential to read all the questions so you can eliminate the two that are most difficult. If, however, you are asked to answer all the questions, there may be danger in trying to answer the easiest one first because you may find that you will spend too much time on it. The best technique is to answer the first question, then proceed to the second, etc.

5) Time your answers. Before the exam begins, write down the time it started, then add the time allowed for the examination and write down the time it must be completed, then divide the time available somewhat as follows:
    - If 3-1/2 hours are allowed, that would be 210 minutes. If you have 80 objective-type questions, that would be an average of 2-1/2 minutes per question. Allow yourself no more than 2 minutes per question, or a total of 160 minutes, which will permit about 50 minutes to review.
    - If for the time allotment of 210 minutes there are 7 essay questions to answer, that would average about 30 minutes a question. Give yourself only 25 minutes per question so that you have about 35 minutes to review.

6) The most important instruction is to *read each question* and make sure you know what is wanted. The second most important instruction is to *time yourself properly* so that you answer every question. The third most important instruction is to *answer every question*. Guess if you have to but include something for each question. Remember that you will receive no credit for a blank and will probably receive some credit if you write something in answer to an essay question. If you guess a letter – say "B" for a multiple-choice question – you may have guessed right. If you leave a blank as an answer to a multiple-choice question, the examiners may respect your feelings but it will not add a point to your score. Some exams may penalize you for wrong answers, so in such cases *only*, you may not want to guess unless you have some basis for your answer.

7) Suggestions
    a. Objective-type questions
        1. Examine the question booklet for proper sequence of pages and questions
        2. Read all instructions carefully
        3. Skip any question which seems too difficult; return to it after all other questions have been answered
        4. Apportion your time properly; do not spend too much time on any single question or group of questions

5. Note and underline key words – *all, most, fewest, least, best, worst, same, opposite,* etc.
6. Pay particular attention to negatives
7. Note unusual option, e.g., unduly long, short, complex, different or similar in content to the body of the question
8. Observe the use of "hedging" words – *probably, may, most likely,* etc.
9. Make sure that your answer is put next to the same number as the question
10. Do not second-guess unless you have good reason to believe the second answer is definitely more correct
11. Cross out original answer if you decide another answer is more accurate; do not erase until you are ready to hand your paper in
12. Answer all questions; guess unless instructed otherwise
13. Leave time for review

b. Essay questions
1. Read each question carefully
2. Determine exactly what is wanted. Underline key words or phrases.
3. Decide on outline or paragraph answer
4. Include many different points and elements unless asked to develop any one or two points or elements
5. Show impartiality by giving pros and cons unless directed to select one side only
6. Make and write down any assumptions you find necessary to answer the questions
7. Watch your English, grammar, punctuation and choice of words
8. Time your answers; don't crowd material

8) Answering the essay question

Most essay questions can be answered by framing the specific response around several key words or ideas. Here are a few such key words or ideas:

M's: manpower, materials, methods, money, management
P's: purpose, program, policy, plan, procedure, practice, problems, pitfalls, personnel, public relations

a. Six basic steps in handling problems:
1. Preliminary plan and background development
2. Collect information, data and facts
3. Analyze and interpret information, data and facts
4. Analyze and develop solutions as well as make recommendations
5. Prepare report and sell recommendations
6. Install recommendations and follow up effectiveness

b. Pitfalls to avoid
1. *Taking things for granted* – A statement of the situation does not necessarily imply that each of the elements is necessarily true; for example, a complaint may be invalid and biased so that all that can be taken for granted is that a complaint has been registered

2. *Considering only one side of a situation* – Wherever possible, indicate several alternatives and then point out the reasons you selected the best one
3. *Failing to indicate follow up* – Whenever your answer indicates action on your part, make certain that you will take proper follow-up action to see how successful your recommendations, procedures or actions turn out to be
4. *Taking too long in answering any single question* – Remember to time your answers properly

IX. AFTER THE TEST

Scoring procedures differ in detail among civil service jurisdictions although the general principles are the same. Whether the papers are hand-scored or graded by machine we have described, they are nearly always graded by number. That is, the person who marks the paper knows only the number – never the name – of the applicant. Not until all the papers have been graded will they be matched with names. If other tests, such as training and experience or oral interview ratings have been given, scores will be combined. Different parts of the examination usually have different weights. For example, the written test might count 60 percent of the final grade, and a rating of training and experience 40 percent. In many jurisdictions, veterans will have a certain number of points added to their grades.

After the final grade has been determined, the names are placed in grade order and an eligible list is established. There are various methods for resolving ties between those who get the same final grade – probably the most common is to place first the name of the person whose application was received first. Job offers are made from the eligible list in the order the names appear on it. You will be notified of your grade and your rank as soon as all these computations have been made. This will be done as rapidly as possible.

People who are found to meet the requirements in the announcement are called "eligibles." Their names are put on a list of eligible candidates. An eligible's chances of getting a job depend on how high he stands on this list and how fast agencies are filling jobs from the list.

When a job is to be filled from a list of eligibles, the agency asks for the names of people on the list of eligibles for that job. When the civil service commission receives this request, it sends to the agency the names of the three people highest on this list. Or, if the job to be filled has specialized requirements, the office sends the agency the names of the top three persons who meet these requirements from the general list.

The appointing officer makes a choice from among the three people whose names were sent to him. If the selected person accepts the appointment, the names of the others are put back on the list to be considered for future openings.

That is the rule in hiring from all kinds of eligible lists, whether they are for typist, carpenter, chemist, or something else. For every vacancy, the appointing officer has his choice of any one of the top three eligibles on the list. This explains why the person whose name is on top of the list sometimes does not get an appointment when some of the persons lower on the list do. If the appointing officer chooses the second or third eligible, the No. 1 eligible does not get a job at once, but stays on the list until he is appointed or the list is terminated.

X. HOW TO PASS THE INTERVIEW TEST

The examination for which you applied requires an oral interview test. You have already taken the written test and you are now being called for the interview test – the final part of the formal examination.

You may think that it is not possible to prepare for an interview test and that there are no procedures to follow during an interview. Our purpose is to point out some things you can do in advance that will help you and some good rules to follow and pitfalls to avoid while you are being interviewed.

What is an interview supposed to test?

The written examination is designed to test the technical knowledge and competence of the candidate; the oral is designed to evaluate intangible qualities, not readily measured otherwise, and to establish a list showing the relative fitness of each candidate – as measured against his competitors – for the position sought. Scoring is not on the basis of "right" and "wrong," but on a sliding scale of values ranging from "not passable" to "outstanding." As a matter of fact, it is possible to achieve a relatively low score without a single "incorrect" answer because of evident weakness in the qualities being measured.

Occasionally, an examination may consist entirely of an oral test – either an individual or a group oral. In such cases, information is sought concerning the technical knowledges and abilities of the candidate, since there has been no written examination for this purpose. More commonly, however, an oral test is used to supplement a written examination.

Who conducts interviews?

The composition of oral boards varies among different jurisdictions. In nearly all, a representative of the personnel department serves as chairman. One of the members of the board may be a representative of the department in which the candidate would work. In some cases, "outside experts" are used, and, frequently, a businessman or some other representative of the general public is asked to serve. Labor and management or other special groups may be represented. The aim is to secure the services of experts in the appropriate field.

However the board is composed, it is a good idea (and not at all improper or unethical) to ascertain in advance of the interview who the members are and what groups they represent. When you are introduced to them, you will have some idea of their backgrounds and interests, and at least you will not stutter and stammer over their names.

What should be done before the interview?

While knowledge about the board members is useful and takes some of the surprise element out of the interview, there is other preparation which is more substantive. It *is* possible to prepare for an oral interview – in several ways:

1) Keep a copy of your application and review it carefully before the interview

This may be the only document before the oral board, and the starting point of the interview. Know what education and experience you have listed there, and the sequence and dates of all of it. Sometimes the board will ask you to review the highlights of your experience for them; you should not have to hem and haw doing it.

2) Study the class specification and the examination announcement

Usually, the oral board has one or both of these to guide them. The qualities, characteristics or knowledges required by the position sought are stated in these documents. They offer valuable clues as to the nature of the oral interview. For example, if the job involves supervisory responsibilities, the announcement will usually indicate that knowledge of modern supervisory methods and the qualifications of the candidate as a supervisor will be tested. If so, you can expect such questions, frequently in the form of a hypothetical situation which you are expected to solve. NEVER go into an oral without knowledge of the duties and responsibilities of the job you seek.

3) Think through each qualification required

Try to visualize the kind of questions you would ask if you were a board member. How well could you answer them? Try especially to appraise your own knowledge and background in each area, *measured against the job sought*, and identify any areas in which you are weak. Be critical and realistic – do not flatter yourself.

4) Do some general reading in areas in which you feel you may be weak

For example, if the job involves supervision and your past experience has NOT, some general reading in supervisory methods and practices, particularly in the field of human relations, might be useful. Do NOT study agency procedures or detailed manuals. The oral board will be testing your understanding and capacity, not your memory.

5) Get a good night's sleep and watch your general health and mental attitude

You will want a clear head at the interview. Take care of a cold or any other minor ailment, and of course, no hangovers.

What should be done on the day of the interview?

Now comes the day of the interview itself. Give yourself plenty of time to get there. Plan to arrive somewhat ahead of the scheduled time, particularly if your appointment is in the fore part of the day. If a previous candidate fails to appear, the board might be ready for you a bit early. By early afternoon an oral board is almost invariably behind schedule if there are many candidates, and you may have to wait. Take along a book or magazine to read, or your application to review, but leave any extraneous material in the waiting room when you go in for your interview. In any event, relax and compose yourself.

The matter of dress is important. The board is forming impressions about you – from your experience, your manners, your attitude, and your appearance. Give your personal appearance careful attention. Dress your best, but not your flashiest. Choose conservative, appropriate clothing, and be sure it is immaculate. This is a business interview, and your appearance should indicate that you regard it as such. Besides, being well groomed and properly dressed will help boost your confidence.

Sooner or later, someone will call your name and escort you into the interview room. *This is it.* From here on you are on your own. It is too late for any more preparation. But remember, you asked for this opportunity to prove your fitness, and you are here because your request was granted.

What happens when you go in?

The usual sequence of events will be as follows: The clerk (who is often the board stenographer) will introduce you to the chairman of the oral board, who will introduce you to the other members of the board. Acknowledge the introductions before you sit down. Do not be surprised if you find a microphone facing you or a stenotypist sitting by. Oral interviews are usually recorded in the event of an appeal or other review.

Usually the chairman of the board will open the interview by reviewing the highlights of your education and work experience from your application – primarily for the benefit of the other members of the board, as well as to get the material into the record. Do not interrupt or comment unless there is an error or significant misinterpretation; if that is the case, do not hesitate. But do not quibble about insignificant matters. Also, he will usually ask you some question about your education, experience or your present job – partly to get you to start talking and to establish the interviewing "rapport." He may start the actual questioning, or turn it over to one of the other members. Frequently, each member undertakes the questioning on a particular area, one in which he is perhaps most competent, so you can expect each member to participate in the examination. Because time is limited, you may also expect some rather abrupt switches in the direction the questioning takes, so do not be upset by it. Normally, a board member will not pursue a single line of questioning unless he discovers a particular strength or weakness.

After each member has participated, the chairman will usually ask whether any member has any further questions, then will ask you if you have anything you wish to add. Unless you are expecting this question, it may floor you. Worse, it may start you off on an extended, extemporaneous speech. The board is not usually seeking more information. The question is principally to offer you a last opportunity to present further qualifications or to indicate that you have nothing to add. So, if you feel that a significant qualification or characteristic has been overlooked, it is proper to point it out in a sentence or so. Do not compliment the board on the thoroughness of their examination – they have been sketchy, and you know it. If you wish, merely say, "No thank you, I have nothing further to add." This is a point where you can "talk yourself out" of a good impression or fail to present an important bit of information. Remember, *you close the interview yourself.*

The chairman will then say, "That is all, Mr. _____, thank you." Do not be startled; the interview is over, and quicker than you think. Thank him, gather your belongings and take your leave. Save your sigh of relief for the other side of the door.

How to put your best foot forward

Throughout this entire process, you may feel that the board individually and collectively is trying to pierce your defenses, seek out your hidden weaknesses and embarrass and confuse you. Actually, this is not true. They are obliged to make an appraisal of your qualifications for the job you are seeking, and they want to see you in your best light. Remember, they must interview all candidates and a non-cooperative candidate may become a failure in spite of their best efforts to bring out his qualifications. Here are 15 suggestions that will help you:

1) Be natural – Keep your attitude confident, not cocky

If you are not confident that you can do the job, do not expect the board to be. Do not apologize for your weaknesses, try to bring out your strong points. The board is interested in a positive, not negative, presentation. Cockiness will antagonize any board member and make him wonder if you are covering up a weakness by a false show of strength.

2) Get comfortable, but don't lounge or sprawl

Sit erectly but not stiffly. A careless posture may lead the board to conclude that you are careless in other things, or at least that you are not impressed by the importance of the occasion. Either conclusion is natural, even if incorrect. Do not fuss with your clothing, a pencil or an ashtray. Your hands may occasionally be useful to emphasize a point; do not let them become a point of distraction.

3) Do not wisecrack or make small talk

This is a serious situation, and your attitude should show that you consider it as such. Further, the time of the board is limited – they do not want to waste it, and neither should you.

4) Do not exaggerate your experience or abilities

In the first place, from information in the application or other interviews and sources, the board may know more about you than you think. Secondly, you probably will not get away with it. An experienced board is rather adept at spotting such a situation, so do not take the chance.

5) If you know a board member, do not make a point of it, yet do not hide it

Certainly you are not fooling him, and probably not the other members of the board. Do not try to take advantage of your acquaintanceship – it will probably do you little good.

6) Do not dominate the interview

Let the board do that. They will give you the clues – do not assume that you have to do all the talking. Realize that the board has a number of questions to ask you, and do not try to take up all the interview time by showing off your extensive knowledge of the answer to the first one.

7) Be attentive

You only have 20 minutes or so, and you should keep your attention at its sharpest throughout. When a member is addressing a problem or question to you, give him your undivided attention. Address your reply principally to him, but do not exclude the other board members.

8) Do not interrupt

A board member may be stating a problem for you to analyze. He will ask you a question when the time comes. Let him state the problem, and wait for the question.

9) Make sure you understand the question

Do not try to answer until you are sure what the question is. If it is not clear, restate it in your own words or ask the board member to clarify it for you. However, do not haggle about minor elements.

10) Reply promptly but not hastily

A common entry on oral board rating sheets is "candidate responded readily," or "candidate hesitated in replies." Respond as promptly and quickly as you can, but do not jump to a hasty, ill-considered answer.

11) Do not be peremptory in your answers

A brief answer is proper – but do not fire your answer back. That is a losing game from your point of view. The board member can probably ask questions much faster than you can answer them.

12) Do not try to create the answer you think the board member wants

He is interested in what kind of mind you have and how it works – not in playing games. Furthermore, he can usually spot this practice and will actually grade you down on it.

13) Do not switch sides in your reply merely to agree with a board member

Frequently, a member will take a contrary position merely to draw you out and to see if you are willing and able to defend your point of view. Do not start a debate, yet do not surrender a good position. If a position is worth taking, it is worth defending.

14) Do not be afraid to admit an error in judgment if you are shown to be wrong

The board knows that you are forced to reply without any opportunity for careful consideration. Your answer may be demonstrably wrong. If so, admit it and get on with the interview.

15) Do not dwell at length on your present job

The opening question may relate to your present assignment. Answer the question but do not go into an extended discussion. You are being examined for a *new* job, not your present one. As a matter of fact, try to phrase ALL your answers in terms of the job for which you are being examined.

Basis of Rating

Probably you will forget most of these "do's" and "don'ts" when you walk into the oral interview room. Even remembering them all will not ensure you a passing grade. Perhaps you did not have the qualifications in the first place. But remembering them will help you to put your best foot forward, without treading on the toes of the board members.

Rumor and popular opinion to the contrary notwithstanding, an oral board wants you to make the best appearance possible. They know you are under pressure – but they also want to see how you respond to it as a guide to what your reaction would be under the pressures of the job you seek. They will be influenced by the degree of poise you display, the personal traits you show and the manner in which you respond.

ABOUT THIS BOOK

This book contains tests divided into Examination Sections. Go through each test, answering every question in the margin. We have also attached a sample answer sheet at the back of the book that can be removed and used. At the end of each test look at the answer key and check your answers. On the ones you got wrong, look at the right answer choice and learn. Do not fill in the answers first. Do not memorize the questions and answers, but understand the answer and principles involved. On your test, the questions will likely be different from the samples. Questions are changed and new ones added. If you understand these past questions you should have success with any changes that arise. Tests may consist of several types of questions. We have additional books on each subject should more study be advisable or necessary for you. Finally, the more you study, the better prepared you will be. This book is intended to be the last thing you study before you walk into the examination room. Prior study of relevant texts is also recommended. NLC publishes some of these in our Fundamental Series. Knowledge and good sense are important factors in passing your exam. Good luck also helps. So now study this Passbook, absorb the material contained within and take that knowledge into the examination. Then do your best to pass that exam.

EXAMINATION SECTION

EXAMINATION SECTION
TEST 1

DIRECTIONS: Each question or incomplete statement is followed by several suggested answers or completions. Select the one that BEST answers the question or completes the statement. *PRINT THE LETTER OF THE CORRECT ANSWER IN THE SPACE AT THE RIGHT.*

1. A listing broker owes a direct fiduciary responsibility to the

    A. buyer's broker
    B. listing salesperson
    C. seller
    D. buyer

    1._____

2. The commission rate for the sale of real estate is determined by

    A. availability of real estate for sale
    B. fixed rates approved by state licensing commissions
    C. negotiation between broker and seller
    D. silent agreement among regional brokers

    2._____

3. In order to be enforceable in court, a sales contract MUST contain

    A. an earnest money deposit
    B. an acknowledgement
    C. a witness
    D. competent parties

    3._____

4. Which of the following, if refused a rental by a singles-only apartment building, would result in a violation of the Federal Fair Housing Act?
A(n)

    A. elderly person
    B. military officer
    C. family
    D. married couple

    4._____

5. A broker USUALLY pays a salesperson a share of the commission received from a sale when

    A. there is a valid and binding offer and acceptance
    B. the sale is closed and the title is transferred to the buyer
    C. the contract and earnest money are placed in escrow
    D. the salesperson submits a sufficient earnest money deposit

    5._____

6. When a broker signs a contract to manage an owner's property, he/she becomes the

    A. receiver   B. fiduciary   C. lessor   D. trustee

    6._____

7. In the death of one of two joint tenants who have taken title to a farm, the

    A. surviving tenant holds title in severalty
    B. surviving tenant holds title subject to the material interest of the deceased's surviving spouse
    C. surviving tenant holds title with the deceased tenant's heirs
    D. deceased tenant's share passes according to his/her will

    7._____

8. If a person sells a home and reinvests the proceeds in the purchase of a new and more expensive home, in order to defer the payment of federal income taxes on any proceeds realized in the sale of the old home the person MUST buy the home within

   A. five years
   B. two years
   C. one year
   D. six months

9. Which of the following is an UNETHICAL practice for a broker representing a seller?

   A. Present written offers that are less than the listing price
   B. Advise a prospective buyer of a cracked foundation
   C. Advise the seller of the highest price a prospective buyer is willing to pay
   D. Advise a prospective buyer of the lowest price the seller is willing to accept

10. A salesperson employed by a real estate broker to show and sell property that is listed with the broker is BEST described as a(n)

    A. principal party to the transaction
    B. agent for the broker who represents the principal
    C. independent contractor
    D. agent for the principal

11. A broker is forbidden from concealing all of the following about a listed property EXCEPT

    A. that the property is located within a flood zone
    B. the type of neighbors who live in the surrounding area
    C. the results of an engineer's environmental hazard report
    D. that a part of the building was constructed without a building permit

12. Under the Federal Fair Housing Act, which of the following is considered discriminatory?

    A. Advertising in the *help wanted* section for a certain race
    B. Rental of property to persons within a certain income bracket
    C. Selling residential land only to Christians
    D. Advertising in the rental section for military personnel only

13. A function of the Truth-In-Lending Law is to

    A. disclose the cost of borrowing
    B. limit the amount of closing costs
    C. limit the amount of interest charged to a borrower
    D. disclose whom the lender represents

14. The phrase *procuring clause* is MOST significant to a seller in relation to a(n)

    A. exclusive-right-to-sell listing
    B. net listing
    C. exclusive agency
    D. open listing

15. The type of listing that gives a broker the GREATEST protection is the _____ listing.

    A. exclusive agency
    B. open
    C. net
    D. exclusive right to sell

16. Which law bars legal claims after certain periods of time?

    A. Administrative Procedures Act
    B. Statute of frauds
    C. Statute of limitations
    D. Real estate law

17. An exclusive element of a sale and leaseback transaction is that the

    A. buyer keeps capital in inventories rather than in realty
    B. rental paid by the seller is not income-tax deductible
    C. property is sold on the condition that the new owner lease it back to the seller when the title passes
    D. seller receives a return on the purchase in the form of rental

18. Which of the following is NOT a function of a mortgage banker?

    A. Lending money and then selling the loan
    B. Preparing an appraisal for a fee
    C. Using his/her own money to make loans
    D. Servicing loans for clients

19. On a settlement statement, the _____ would be a DEBIT to the buyer.

    A. new mortgage
    B. assumed mortgage
    C. purchase price
    D. earnest money deposit

20. Which of the following is a real estate broker NOT usually authorized to do as an agent of the seller?

    A. Advertise listed property
    B. Place a *for sale* sign on the listed property
    C. Cooperate with other brokers to bring about a sale
    D. Bind the principal under a sales contract

21. When a broker obtains a listing

    A. any buyer should be given a copy of the listing
    B. the listing should be prepared in writing
    C. there is no fiduciary relationship between the broker and seller
    D. the seller may legally cancel it at any time

22. A legal reason for offering a SHORTER than normal mortgage term is

    A. physical decrepitude of borrower
    B. short leasehold term
    C. pregnancy of borrower
    D. mental handicap of borrower

23. When a mortgagor is declared bankrupt, the

    A. title passes to a court trustee or receiver
    B. mortgagor no longer owes money under the mortgage note
    C. mortgagee becomes a general creditor
    D. mortgagor retains an equitable title to the property but forfeits the legal title

24. *Right of first refusal* in a lease means that the tenant can

    A. extend
    B. cancel
    C. match an offer to relet
    D. buy at a foreclosure sale

25. A special agent would be BEST described as a(n)

    A. person with limited authority
    B. person with contractual authority
    C. broker
    D. attorney

KEY (CORRECT ANSWERS)

1.	C	11.	B
2.	C	12.	C
3.	D	13.	A
4.	C	14.	D
5.	B	15.	D
6.	B	16.	C
7.	A	17.	C
8.	B	18.	B
9.	D	19.	C
10.	B	20.	D

21. B
22. B
23. D
24. C
25. A

TEST 2

DIRECTIONS: Each question or incomplete statement is followed by several suggested answers or completions. Select the one that BEST answers the question or completes the statement. *PRINT THE LETTER OF THE CORRECT ANSWER IN THE SPACE AT THE RIGHT.*

1. If the terms of a contract have NOT been fully performed, it is defined as

    A. executed
    B. unilateral
    C. executory
    D. bilateral

2. What has MOST likely occurred if the replacement cost shows a HIGHER value than the appraised value?

    A. Accrued depreciation
    B. Economic obsolescence
    C. Excessive appraisal
    D. Capitalization

3. _____ do NOT need to be covered in a properly drawn property management agreement.

    A. Operating expenses
    B. Duration of term
    C. Management fees
    D. Manager's duties

4. The listing property owner is known to a real estate broker as a(n)

    A. fiduciary   B. prospect   C. principal   D. agent

5. A real estate broker is MOST likely to have an agency relationship with

    A. the seller
    B. the buyer
    C. escrow
    D. an attorney

6. A broker may accept commissions from BOTH buyer and seller

    A. if there is a written listing from both
    B. only if the total amount is under $15,000
    C. if both consent after full disclosure
    D. under no circumstances

7. Federal antidiscriminatory laws apply to

    A. private lodging for noncommercial purposes in a private club
    B. sales by broker of single-family homes
    C. sales of office buildings
    D. rentals of industrial property

8. Which of the following documents is NOT usually recorded in a real estate transaction?

    A. Second mortgage
    B. Purchase money mortgage
    C. Deed
    D. Offer to purchase

9. The _____ of the _____ is NOT required for a valid bill of sale.

    A. name; buyer
    B. description; property
    C. signature; seller
    D. date; transaction

10. Which of the following BEST describes the relationship between property owner and broker?

    A. Seller/purchaser
    B. Principal/agent
    C. Attorney/client
    D. Optionor/optionee

11. Which of the following will NOT terminate a listing contract?

    A. Sudden increase in market value
    B. Death of the listing broker
    C. Bankruptcy of the listing broker
    D. Destruction of the listed property

12. A listing contract creates a(n)

    A. agency between the buyer and the broker showing the property
    B. fiduciary agency relationship between broker and seller
    C. special agency relationship between the broker and a salesperson
    D. agency between the buyer and seller

13. Which of the following is NOT a contract?

    A. Listing
    B. Trust deed
    C. Mortgage
    D. Closing statement

14. If an option contract has been duly executed by buyer and seller,

    A. the seller must sell, but the buyer is not required to buy
    B. it is specifically enforceable by both parties
    C. the buyer must buy
    D. the seller is not required to sell

15. The one of the following that is NOT one of a broker's responsibilities in presenting the seller a written offer to purchase is

    A. presenting only the offers that are within 15 percent of the asking price
    B. presenting all written offers to the seller before the seller accepts an offer
    C. exposing and explaining the implications and practical effects of each offer
    D. presenting all offers as rapidly as they are received

16. Which of the following is NOT an action available to a complainant who files a discrimination lawsuit in a federal district court?

    A. Money damages
    B. Permanent injunction
    C. Triple damages
    D. Temporary restraining order

17. _____ should be placed into the general account by a broker acting as property manager.

    A. Security deposits
    B. Rents
    C. Broker's earned commissions
    D. Pet deposits

18. A PROPER escrow, once it has been established, is

    A. managed by a licensed broker
    B. void at the seller's option
    C. not subject to the control of any one interested party
    D. voidable at the option of either buyer or seller

19. The term that SPECIFICALLY describes the situation when a landlord and tenant agree to terminate a lease is

    A. surrender   B. release
    C. abandonment   D. rejection

20. Which of the following should be done by a broker handling a real estate transaction?

    A. Reveal only items requested by the seller
    B. Provide the client with a statement of receipts and disbursements
    C. Conceal building code violations from the client
    D. Reveal only property elements that are part of public record

21. Which of the following does NOT terminate an agency relationship?

    A. Destruction of the subject property
    B. Death of the owner
    C. A written offer
    D. Bankruptcy of the principal broker

22. The MOST essential element for an enforceable real estate contract is

    A. the time of closing   B. being in written form
    C. the date of contract   D. being witnessed

23. An abstract title

    A. guarantees the title
    B. insures the title
    C. covers encroachment
    D. gives a history of the title

24. Which of the following would NOT be a material fact requiring disclosure by the real estate broker?

    A. Leaking roof
    B. Drainage problems
    C. Prior tenant has AIDS
    D. House is not connected to sewage system

25. The subagent of a seller is BEST described as a(n)

    A. general agent   B. buyer's broker
    C. special agent   D. universal agent

KEY (CORRECT ANSWERS)

1.	C	11.	A
2.	A	12.	B
3.	A	13.	D
4.	C	14.	A
5.	A	15.	A
6.	C	16.	C
7.	B	17.	C
8.	D	18.	C
9.	D	19.	A
10.	B	20.	B

21. C
22. B
23. D
24. C
25. C

———

EXAMINATION SECTION
TEST 1

DIRECTIONS: Each question or incomplete statement is followed by several suggested answers or completions. Select the one that BEST answers the question or completes the statement. *PRINT THE LETTER OF THE CORRECT ANSWER IN THE SPACE AT THE RIGHT.*

1. The relationship of real estate brokers and salesmen to their clients is BEST characterized as being governed by the law of
    A. master and servant
    B. principal and agent
    C. principal and owner
    D. all of the above

2. An authorization or contract of employment between a real estate broker or salesman and his client
    A. must always be in writing
    B. must always be specific and detailed
    C. need not be in writing after they have come to an agreement
    D. must be in writing if it is not to be performed within one year

3. The terms of a contract between a broker or salesman and his client
    A. must be specifically agreed to in writing
    B. must be specifically agreed to verbally
    C. can be implied from their actions
    D. can be implied from their actions unless the contract is not to be performed for 1 year

4. A written contract between a real estate broker and his client
    A. must be signed by both parties
    B. must be signed by only the party to be charged
    C. doesn't have to be signed at all
    D. must be signed only by the broker

5. An *open listing* is in effect when a client lists his property
    A. only with one broker exclusively
    B. with many brokers and, when one of them negotiates a sale, the authority of the others is terminated
    C. with many brokers and, after a sale is negotiated by two or more brokers, the seller has an *open* decision as to which one he will accept
    D. none of the above

6. When an owner grants a broker the exclusive right to sell his land, the
    A. broker must sell it or buy it himself
    B. broker has the exclusive right to sell it and, if he is unsuccessful, the owner has no other action than to contract with another broker
    C. owner, himself, also has the right to sell the land and, if he does, he does not have to pay the broker's commission
    D. owner, himself, also has the right to sell the land but, if he does, he must pay his exclusive broker his fee anyway

7. A broker who has the exclusive right to sell an estate

   A. can accept an offer for the set price and have the buyer sign the contract
   B. cannot accept an offer for the set price unless given that authority by the owner
   C. must accept an offer of the set price or a higher price but must wait until the owner is present before the buyer signs
   D. can act as if he were the owner of the property

8. The employment of a real estate broker

   A. must last for a specified time
   B. lasts until the broker negotiates a sale
   C. may be set definitely or not, but the broker must be notified of termination
   D. cannot be terminated until the end of the period of time set

9. Where a fixed time is set for the broker's employment, the owner

   A. cannot terminate his employment until that period of time has expired
   B. is answerable to the broker in damages if he cancels the broker's authority prior to the expiration date of the broker's agency
   C. can terminate the broker's employment at will and is not liable in damages
   D. can terminate the broker's employment only if he has negotiated a sale himself

10. Which of the following is(are) a valid reason for the termination of the broker's authority?
    I. When the object has not been performed during the specified period or, where the period of authority is unspecified, the object has not been performed or accomplished within a reasonable time
    II. The death or insanity of a broker or principal
    III. The bankruptcy of a broker or principal
    IV. The destruction of the subject matter
    V. The broker's fraudulent conduct for his own benefit
    VI. The sale by another broker if the authority is for an unspecified time
    The CORRECT answer is:

    A. I only
    B. I, II, V
    C. I, II, IV, V, VI
    D. All of the above

11. The employment of the same broker by both the seller and the buyer

    A. is a misdemeanor
    B. violates the broker's duty and constitutes a conflict of interest
    C. is grounds for a principal to withhold the broker's commission
    D. is permitted, and neither principal may withhold compensation if he knew or consented to the dual employment

12. A and B contracted for the sale of a piece of real estate situated in Florida at B's broker's office in New York. As A was about to take possession, a conflict arose between A and B as to a provision of their agreement.
    To clarify the agreement, the law of which state should be applied?

    A. New York
    B. Florida
    C. Either Florida or New York
    D. The state in which B's broker is licensed

13. A broker is entitled to a commission when

    A. he introduces the ultimate purchaser to the seller
    B. the minds of the seller and buyer meet as to price although they may still be in disagreement in other respects
    C. the minds of the seller and buyer meet as to all terms of the sale
    D. he helps another broker close a deal although he is not the procuring cause of the sale

14. Which of the following terms is(are) essential to effect a meeting of the minds?
    I. Price
    II. Duration of mortgages
    III. Amount of cash
    IV. Amortization
    V. Rate of interest

    The CORRECT answer is:

    A. I, II, III, IV, V   B. I *only*   C. I, III, V   D. I, II, III, V

15. Which of the following statements MOST correctly describes the commission rate charged by a real estate broker?

    A. The commission rates adopted by a real estate board govern all commissions earned in that community.
    B. The commission rates of a real estate broker are fixed by statute.
    C. The commission rates adopted by a real estate board, if generally accepted by the public, create a customary rate of compensation which the courts will enforce in the absence of a specific agreement between the broker and his employer.
    D. In the absence of a written agreement between a broker and his employer, the broker must earn the commission at the rate set by the real estate board.

16. If an owner employs more than one broker independently of one another,

    A. each broker is entitled to the same compensation when the deal is closed
    B. each broker is entitled to some compensation but the broker who actually negotiated the transaction is entitled to more
    C. the broker who first induces the customer to agree to the owner's terms gets the entire commission, the other brokers receive nothing
    D. the broker who actually negotiates the sale forfeits his right to compensation if the employer mistakenly pays another broker a full commission on the same transaction

17. To be entitled to his commission, the broker must produce a customer who is *ready, willing, and able.*
    This phrase means MOST NEARLY: The customer

    A. is prepared to sign a contract with the broker's principal after the negotiation of some minor details
    B. has signed the contract with the broker's principal but must prove his ability to pay
    C. is ready to sign the contract and does not have to tender any sums of money until he takes ownership
    D. is ready to sign the contract on the principal's terms and is either prepared to tender the sums or deeds required at the time of the execution of the contract or can prove his ability to pay if the contract has not yet been signed

18. When the broker has a customer for his client's property,

    A. the broker is under an obligation to disclose the customer's identity to his client so that the client can investigate him
    B. the broker may lose his commission if the customer later goes directly to the owner and negotiates a sale if the broker originally did not reveal the identity of the customer to the client
    C. the broker is entitled to the commission although the customer later deals directly with the owner notwithstanding that the broker had not revealed the customer's name to the owner
    D. he is not required to disclose the customer's name even though the client may request it

19. A broker's commission is payable

    A. in advance of his services so as to mitigate his personal expenditures
    B. only when he produces a customer who is ready, willing, and able to buy on the specified terms in the listing
    C. when he produces a customer who is *ready, willing, and able* after bargaining with his client although the mutually agreed-to terms differ from that of the listing
    D. when the customer takes ownership

20. After a broker has fulfilled the terms of his employment,

    A. he must be paid his commission even though the transactions might later fail because of a defect in title
    B. the broker can orally waive the payment of his commission if the transaction fails and this will be enforceable in court against the broker
    C. the broker must waive his commission in writing for it to be enforceable in court
    D. the broker must waive his commission in writing for it to be binding in court and, where the broker's employer was at fault for the nonconsummation of the transaction, the court usually will not hold the broker to his waiver

21. Under which combination of the following circumstances is the broker entitled to his commission?
    Where
    I. a purchaser refuses to take title because of ordinary street encroachments
    II. an owner refuses to sign a contract of sale on the terms he originally proposed
    III. an owner misrepresents the size of his property or the amount of rentals
    IV. the owner terminates a broker's employment to be able to sell or lease directly

    The CORRECT answer is:

    A. I, III, IV   B. II, III, IV   C. I, II, III, IV   D. II, III

22. Under which combination of the following circumstances is the broker entitled to a commission?　22.____
    I. When the customer has signed a binder to pay the broker's commission and the customer fails or refuses to consummate the negotiation
    II. Where the customer has signed a binder to pay the broker's commission and the transaction is not closed because the seller's title is defective
    III. After the contract has been entered into by the buyer and seller and the customer fails to complete the purchases, for inability, refusal or failure to perform
    IV. Where the customer is ready, willing, but not financially able to perform
    The CORRECT answer is:

    A. I, II, III, IV
    B. I, II, III
    C. I, II
    D. I only

23. The relationship of the real estate broker to his client is such that it requires that the　23.____

    A. client may hold his agent to strict loyalty and require him to account fully for the profits of a transaction wherein the client was defrauded
    B. broker disclose every higher offer of purchase to the client
    C. broker reveal any facts in his possession concerning the purchaser's intention to resell and the broker's own interest in the purchase, should he or a partnership or corporation of which he is a part have one
    D. all of the above

24. The duty of a broker to a customer or prospective purchaser is characterized as　24.____

    A. an agent-principal relationship
    B. essentially negative; any misstatement or misrepresentation by the broker to the customer about the client's property is fraud and hence a good defense for the owner to the broker's claim for commission and a justification for the purchaser to refuse to take title
    C. essentially positive; the customer is as much the broker's client as is the owner so that the broker is expected to work on the customer's behalf against the owner as he is expected to work for the owner
    D. none of the above

25. Which group of the following statements is TRUE?　25.____
    I. The listing of a parcel of real property with a broker confers upon the broker the authority to accept a deposit from a prospective purchaser.
    II. If a real estate broker, in conjunction with the receipt of an offer of purchase, undertakes to accept a deposit from the prospective purchaser, he does so on his own, and the receipt of such deposit by the broker has no binding effect insofar as the owner is concerned.
    III. The broker becomes the agent of the purchaser when he accepts the deposit to turn over to the seller should he accept the purchaser's offer, and the deposit remains the property of the purchaser until the seller accepts the offer.

IV. It is unlawful for the broker to induce the buyer to make the deposit by assuring him that the deposit will be returned in the event that a mortgage loan is not obtained, and such clause, incorporated in the contract, is not valid.
V. Where the buyer is capable of fulfilling the condition of the contract, but the completion of the transaction is frustrated by a defect in the seller's title, the broker is not entitled to keep the buyer's deposit.
VI. The monies placed with the brokers are in trust, cannot be commingled with the broker's personal funds, and must be kept in a separate, special bank account.

The CORRECT answer is:

A. I, II, III, IV, V, VI
B. I, III, IV, V
C. II, III, VI
D. II, III, IV, VI

KEY (CORRECT ANSWERS)

1.	B	11.	D
2.	D	12.	A
3.	D	13.	C
4.	B	14.	A
5.	B	15.	C
6.	D	16.	C
7.	B	17.	D
8.	C	18.	B
9.	B	19.	C
10.	D	20.	D

21.	B
22.	B
23.	D
24.	B
25.	C

TEST 2

DIRECTIONS: Each question or incomplete statement is followed by several suggested answers or completions. Select the one that BEST answers the question or completes the statement. *PRINT THE LETTER OF THE CORRECT ANSWER IN THE SPACE AT THE RIGHT.*

1. Which combination of the following statements is FALSE?   1.____
    I. *Exclusive Listing* is the same as *Exclusive Right* to sell.
    II. Only attorneys at law may hold a valid power of attorney.
    III. A listing contract is terminated by the death of the principal.
    IV. If two parties to an escrow make conflicting demands upon the escrow holder, he may refuse to act further until an agreement has been reached or until the courts have directed the disposition of the instruments and money deposited in the escrow.
    The CORRECT answer is:

    A. I, II, III   B. I, II, IV
    C. I, II   D. II, III, IV

2. Which combination of the following statements is TRUE?   2.____
    I. The terms *option* and *listing* have the same meaning.
    II. Open listing means the price is not set.
    III. An exclusive listing cannot be terminated.
    IV. An open listing is more advantageous to a broker than an exclusive listing.
    The CORRECT answer is:

    A. I, II, IV   B. None of the above
    C. I, IV   D. IV *only*

3. Which combination of the following statements is TRUE?   3.____
    I. A listing gives authority to sell.
    II. A realtor is an active member of a local real estate board affiliated with the National Association of Real Estate Boards.
    III. Giving a broker the exclusive right of sale binds the owner to pay a commission to the broker even if the owner sells the property himself.
    IV. Commission rates are not established by law but are a matter between the client and his agent.
    The CORRECT answer is:

    A. I, II, III   B. I, II, III, IV
    C. II, III, IV   D. II, III

4. A listing is   4.____

    A. an option
    B. a land contract
    C. property for sale
    D. the broker's contract of employment with an owner to find a purchaser for the owner's property

5. A written agreement giving the agent a right to collect a commission, no matter who sells the property, is a(n)

   A. option
   B. open listing
   C. exclusive right to sell
   D. multiple listing

6. A contract which provides for the payment of a commission to a broker, even though the owner makes the sale without the aid of the broker, is called

   A. exclusive listing
   B. open listing
   C. exclusive right to sell
   D. option

7. All listings should be taken in the name of

   A. buyer
   B. seller
   C. salesman (licensed)
   D. principal licensed broker

8. A power of attorney is terminated by

   A. an express revocation by the principal
   B. the death of the principal
   C. incapability of the principal to contract
   D. any of the above

9. When a broker receives a deposit on a business which he has listed, the money becomes the property of the

   A. seller
   B. broker
   C. escrow company
   D. prospective buyers

10. When the purchaser is ready, willing, and able to buy, the broker, to bind the transaction, should take a

    A. mortgage
    B. trust deed
    C. deposit
    D. contract of sale

11. Which combination of the following statements is TRUE?
    I. In closing sales and leases, the broker should always recommend the employment of competent legal counsel.
    II. The proper fees of attorneys are paid by both the buyer and the seller.
    III. A broker should always consult an attorney before signing any listing agreement.
    IV. An attorney is superfluous when a real estate broker is present.
    The CORRECT answer is:

    A. I, II
    B. I, III
    C. I, II, III
    D. None of the above

12. Which combination of the following statements is FALSE?   12.____
    I.   It is good policy for a broker to give a copy of the listing agreement to the owner who employs him.
    II. A real estate salesman may be lawfully employed by, and may accept compensation from, any broker other than the broker under whom he is licensed.
    III. Where a real estate salesman employed by one broker is assisted in a transaction by a real estate salesman employed by another broker, under an arrangement whereby both salesmen are to have a part of the commission, it is lawful for the first to pay directly to the second salesman the latter's share of the commission.
    IV. If, after a listing is taken, an earnest money receipt signed, or a contract executed, a slight change is made in the terms or conditions, and the broker, in the presence of the interested parties, alters the writing to conform to the new arrangement, the broker should have all parties place their signatures or initials in the margin opposite the alteration.

    The CORRECT answer is:

    A. I, III   B. II, IV
    C. II, III   D. All of the above

13. Which combination of the following statements is TRUE?   13.____
    I.   When a real estate broker who is employed to sell a particular property buys it himself, but in the name of a *dummy,* the sale will stand if attacked.
    II. A broker is employed by an owner to sell a particular property. He introduces a prospective purchaser to the owner who, a short time later, cancels the contract of employment. Some time later, the owner sells to this prospect. The broker is not entitled to his commission.
    III. A real estate broker is probably liable for frauds and misrepresentations of a salesman working out of his office even though the broker had no knowledge of the misrepresentations and did not participate in them.
    IV. A real estate broker is not liable to third persons for the misrepresentation of the broker with whom he is associated unless he participates in the fraud.

    The CORRECT answer is:

    A. I, III   B. II, III, IV
    C. III, IV   D. I, II, III, IV

14. Which combination of the following statements is TRUE?   14.____
    I.   It is necessary that a contract employing a real estate broker to sell real estate for commission be in writing.
    II. The Statute of Frauds is usually strictly interpreted against the broker by the courts.
    III. A broker who accepts oral employment to sell real estate, and then finds a purchaser who buys the property and pays the owner his full asking price, is helpless to recover compensation.
    IV. If a real estate broker is merely orally employed to sell real estate; finds a purchaser to whom he gives a receipt for the earnest money; and then secures the owner's written approval of the sale and the latter's written agreement to pay a commission, the broker is still not entitled to a commission because of the Statute of Frauds.

    The CORRECT answer is:

    A. I, II   B. I, II, III
    C. I, II, IV   D. I, II, III, IV

15. Which combination of the following statements is FALSE?
    I. There is no difference between an exclusive right to sell and an exclusive agency listing.
    II. If a husband employs a real estate broker to sell property and the broker procures a purchaser ready, willing, and able to buy on the husband's exact terms but the wife refuses to sign the deed so that the sale is never consummated, the broker can still collect his commission from the husband.
    III. If a person with no legal interest in a property employs a broker who finds a purchaser ready, willing, and able to buy but the sale cannot be consummated, the broker cannot get a commission.
    IV. A broker can recover no commission for services in bringing about a sale of real estate where his contract of employment does not specify the amount thereof.

    The CORRECT answer is:

    A. I, III
    B. I, IV
    C. I, II, III
    D. I, II, III, IV

16. Which combination of the following statements is FALSE?
    I. A broker may never receive compensation from both parties to the same transaction.
    II. When a real estate broker with no written contract for commission brings about an exchange of properties and the parties to the exchange agree in their contract with each other to pay a commission, the broker can recover that commission.
    III. When an owner refuses to sell his property to a buyer brought in by a broker who has deposited with the broker earnest money to bind the sale, the broker may keep the earnest money as his commission and the owner must repay the amount of the earnest money to the prospect.
    IV. It is correct practice for a salesman to complete a sale and collect in his own name the commission and then give his broker-employer his share of the commission.

    The CORRECT answer is:

    A. I, IV
    B. II, III
    C. I, II, III
    D. I, II, III, IV

17. Which combination of the following statements is TRUE?
    I. When earnest money is received by a salesman, he is at liberty to make use of it for his personal account up to the amount of his share of the commission before the deal is closed.
    II. It is legal for a broker to place a sign on property without the consent of the owner.
    III. If a broker is assisted by his grocer in procuring a prospect or in closing a deal, it is lawful for the broker to pay the grocer for his services a fair and reasonable portion of his commission.
    IV. It is lawful for a broker to agree with a tenant of the house which the broker has for sale to pay the tenant a portion of the commission should a prospect to whom the tenant shows the property later buy the same.

    The CORRECT answer is:

    A. I, III, IV
    B. II, III
    C. III, IV
    D. None of the above

18. Which combination of the following statements is FALSE?
   I. It is lawful for a broker to pay any third person a stated sum for services rendered in connection with showing the property or assisting in a real estate transaction.
   II. A broker's or salesman's license may be revoked for guaranteeing or promising to a prospective purchaser a definite quick profit on the resale of the property.
   III. The real estate commissioner has the power to compel a broker or salesman to make restitution in cases of fraud and misrepresentation.
   IV. *Consideration,* when used in reference to a real estate contract, is synonymous with the word *inducement.*
   The CORRECT answer is:

   A. I, II
   B. I, III
   C. II, IV
   D. I, II, III, IV

19. Which combination of the following statements is FALSE?
   I. A special agent is more limited in his authority than a general agent.
   II. A special agent usually is retained for a single transaction for his principal.
   III. A real estate broker is an example of a general agent.
   IV. A store manager is an example of a special agent.
   The CORRECT answer is:

   A. I, II   B. I, III   C. III, IV   D. II, IV

20. Which combination of the following statements is TRUE?
   I. Agency is usually created by a contract.
   II. In the case of a real estate broker, the agency agreement is the listing contract.
   III. The listing agreement must be exclusive listing in order for an agency agreement to exist.
   IV. A listing agreement is merely an employment contract.
   The CORRECT answer is:

   A. I, II
   B. I, II, IV
   C. I, III
   D. I, II, III, IV

21. Which combination of the following statements is FALSE?
   I. The authority of the agent to act for his principal is usually given to him by the terms of the agency agreement.
   II. The agent's authority may be either *actual* or *apparent*.
   III. Actual authority is far more common than apparent authority.
   IV. Actual authority may either be expressed or implied.
   The CORRECT answer is:

   A. III *only*
   B. II, IV
   C. I, III, IV
   D. None of the above

22. An agent's express authority is

   A. given to him by the conduct of the principal
   B. given to him orally
   C. given to him in writing
   D. characterized by all of the above

23. Which of the following is an example of a real estate broker's implied authority as an agent?

   A. Signing a listing contract
   B. Hiring a salesman
   C. Putting an advertisement in the newspaper
   D. All of the above

24. Which of the following statements concerning an agent's delegation of authority to a sub-agent is CORRECT?
   A real estate

   A. agent has no authority to delegate that authority to a sub-agent
   B. broker's implied authority to delegate his authority to a salesman derives from custom and usage
   C. broker has an express authority to delegate his authority to a salesman
   D. broker never delegates his authority to a salesman

25. An agent's apparent authority

   A. is different from his implied or expressed authority
   B. is an outgrowth of his relations to third parties
   C. will bind third persons who relied on it so they can hold his principal liable for the agent's acts
   D. is characterized by all of the above

KEY (CORRECT ANSWERS)

1.	C	11.	A
2.	B	12.	C
3.	B	13.	C
4.	D	14.	B
5.	C	15.	A
6.	C	16.	D
7.	D	17.	D
8.	D	18.	B
9.	A	19.	C
10.	C	20.	B

21. D
22. D
23. C
24. B
25. D

TEST 3

DIRECTIONS: Each question or incomplete statement is followed by several suggested answers or completions. Select the one that BEST answers the question or completes the statement. *PRINT THE LETTER OF THE CORRECT ANSWER IN THE SPACE AT THE RIGHT.*

1. Which combination of the following duties does the principal owe to his agent? To
    I. perform the agency contract
    II. compensate the agent
    III. reimburse the agent for expenses
    IV. indemnify the agent for loss suffered because of the agency
   The CORRECT answer is:

   A. I, II
   B. I, II, III
   C. II *only*
   D. All of the above

   1._____

2. Which combination of the following is TRUE?
    I. The principal and agent each have the duty to abide by the terms of the contract.
    II. If the principal wrongfully breaks the contract, the agency is terminated.
    III. If the principal wrongfully breaks the contract, he will be liable in damages to the agent.
    IV. If the agent is guilty of wrongdoing, then the principal may terminate the agency without incurring any liability.
   The CORRECT answer is:

   A. I *only*
   B. I, III
   C. II, III, IV
   D. All of the above

   2._____

3. Which combination of the following statements is FALSE?
    I. Neither the principal nor agent may interfere with the performance of the contract by the other.
    II. When the agent has performed his part of the agreement, the principal has the duty to pay him the amount of money agreed upon.
    III. If no amount of compensation is agreed to or stated, the principal must pay the agent what he demands.
    IV. If the agent incurs expenses in performing authorized acts for the principal, the agent incurs the expense as part of his operating expenses.
   The CORRECT answer is:

   A. I, III
   B. III, IV
   C. II, IV
   D. All of the above

   3._____

4. Which of the following are duties owed by the agent to his principal? To
    I. perform the agency agreement
    II. be loyal to his principal
    III. use reasonable care in performing the agency
    IV. account for all money and property received
    V. perform acts in person
   The CORRECT answer is:

   A. I, IV
   B. I, II, III, IV
   C. I, II, III
   D. All of the above

   4._____

21

5. Which combination of the following statements is TRUE? The agent
   I. owes a duty of loyalty and trust to his principal
   II. may personally profit from the agency relationship in any lawful way as well as receive his commission
   III. has a duty after the agency relationship is terminated not to divulge all material confidential information obtained as a result of his agency
   IV. can be held responsible for any loss caused by his disobedience to his principal's instructions

   The CORRECT answer is:

   A. I, II, III
   B. I, III, IV
   C. I, II
   D. All of the above

6. Which combination of the following statements is FALSE?
   I. An agent may not have interests opposed to his principal.
   II. An agent may represent another who has adverse interests to his principal if he has his principal's consent.
   III. The agent has no duty to tell his principal all matters within his realm of knowledge pertaining to the property.
   IV. A real estate broker can purchase property for himself with his client's consent.

   The CORRECT answer is:

   A. III, IV
   B. III *only*
   C. II, III, IV
   D. I, II, IV

7. Which combination of the following statements is TRUE?
   I. The broker can withhold an offer to purchase because he fears a new offer, which is only slightly higher, might upset a current deal.
   II. The agent must use his best efforts to obtain the most advantageous deal for his principal.
   III. If the agent fails to inform his principal, he can be held liable for loss resulting to the principal.
   IV. A real estate broker can't be penalized for neglecting to inform his client of a change in the zoning ordinance.

   The CORRECT answer is:

   A. II, III
   B. I, III, IV
   C. II, III, IV
   D. All of the above

8. Which combination of the following statements is TRUE?
   I. The agent can be held liable to the principal for any loss caused by his lack of care.
   II. An agent holding himself out to the public as possessing certain skills has a duty to use the care of a competent person having such skills.
   III. The level of competence is measured by a comparison with that of other brokers in the state.
   IV. A broker can escape responsibility for his negligence by pleading ignorance.

   The CORRECT answer is:

   A. I, II, III
   B. I, II, III, IV
   C. I, II
   D. None of the above

9. Which combination of the following statements is FALSE? 9.____
    I. The agent has the duty to make an accounting to his principal for all money or other valuable consideration which he receives in the course of the agency.
    II. The agent must keep accurate records and accounts of all transactions.
    III. The broker must segregate the funds of his principal from his own.
    IV. The real estate broker should deposit in a separate trust account funds received from the buyer as part payment on the purchase of real estate.
    The CORRECT answer is:

    A. I, IV
    C. II, III
    B. III, IV
    D. None of the above

10. Which combination of the following statements is TRUE? 10.____
    I. Funds received by a salesman may be deposited by him.
    II. The salesman must keep all copies of the material documents of the transaction.
    III. It is not at all times necessary for the listing broker to handle all facets of the transaction himself.
    IV. The duty to perform acts in person is a qualified obligation.
    The CORRECT answer is:

    A. I, III, IV
    C. I, II, III
    B. III, IV
    D. All of the above

11. Which combination of the following statements is FALSE? 11.____
    I. If the principal so designates, the transaction cannot be performed by anyone other than the agent selected.
    II. In the case of real estate brokers, it is usually understood or implied that sub-agents may be employed.
    III. A real estate broker may delegate part of the transaction to a multiple listing service of which he is not the owner.
    IV. The broker's basic legal obligation is superseded by the sub-agent used.
    The CORRECT answer is:

    A. IV *only*
    C. I, III, IV
    B. I, III
    D. I, II, III

12. Which combination of the following statements is FALSE? 12.____
    I. If the agent has authority to enter into a contract with a third party on behalf of the principal, the agent has no personal responsibility to perform such a contract.
    II. If the principal fails or refuses to perform, the agent cannot be held liable for the principal's non-performance.
    III. If the agent enters into a contract for his principal without, in some way, revealing that he is an agent, he can be held personally liable for the performance of the contract by the third party.
    IV. If the agent enters into a contract for his principal without revealing that he is an agent, he may hold the third party responsible for performance.
    The CORRECT answer is:

    A. I, IV
    C. III, IV
    B. I, II, IV
    D. None of the above

13. Which combination of the following statements is TRUE?
    I. A real estate broker has no authority to sign a contract for the sale of real estate.
    II. A real estate broker has authority only to find a ready, willing, and able purchaser to buy on terms set forth by the seller.
    III. After a broker has found a ready, willing, and able purchaser and the owner fails or refuses to perform the contract of sale, the broker is liable to the buyer.
    IV. If a person claims to be an agent for another, he implicitly warrants or guarantees that he has such authority.
    The CORRECT answer is:

    A. I, III
    B. I, II, III
    C. I, II, IV
    D. All of the above

14. Which combination of the following statements is TRUE?
    I. An agent is personally responsible to the third party for any tort which he might commit, whether with or without his principal's permission.
    II. If a real estate broker or salesman knowingly misrepresents a material fact concerning the property for the purpose of inducing the prospect to purchase and the prospect does no purchase, relying on the misrepresentation, the agent is responsible for the tort of fraud or deceit.
    III. If the agent defrauded the purchaser with the principal's consent, the purchaser has the choice of recovering the loss from the agent or the principal.
    IV. A third party is liable to the agent for any tort he may commit against the principal.
    The CORRECT answer is:

    A. I, II
    B. I, II, III
    C. I, III, IV
    D. All of the above

15. Which combination of the following statements is FALSE?
    I. The principal owes the duty to the third person of performing contracts made by his authorized agent.
    II. If the principal does not perform, the third party may hold him liable for breach of contract.
    III. The third party is responsible to the agent for performing contracts made with the agent.
    IV. In the usual real estate situation, the buyer and seller personally sign the contract.
    The CORRECT answer is:

    A. I, III
    B. II, IV
    C. III *only*
    D. None of the above

16. Which combination of the following statements is FALSE?
    I. The principal is personally liable for the torts of his agent if he authorized the agent to do the wrongful act or if the act was within the scope of the agent's employment.
    II. A seller of real estate is liable to the buyer for the false representation as to a material fact about the property made by the broker or salesman which induced the purchaser to buy, if such representation was with either the seller's knowledge or his express or implied consent.
    III. It is good practice for the broker to make a careful investigation of the property before offering it for sale.
    IV. A broker or salesman might be held liable for negligence if he fails to inform himself of the facts which a reasonable inquiry might disclose.
    The CORRECT answer is:

    A. I, IV
    B. II, IV
    C. II, III, IV
    D. None of the above

17. Which combination of the following statements is TRUE?
    I. The parties to the agency agreement, by either their rightful or wrongful action, may voluntarily terminate the agency.
    II. The principal and the agent may by mutual agreement put an end to the agency relationship at any time.
    III. The agency agreement itself usually sets the time of termination.
    IV. If the agreement calls for the accomplishment of a particular object, the agency ends when that object has been accomplished.
    The CORRECT answer is:

    A. I, II, IV
    B. II, IV
    C. IV *only*
    D. All of the above

18. Which combination of the following statements is FALSE?
    I. If no termination date is specified in the contract, it is generally implied that the agency is for a reasonable period of time under the circumstances.
    II. The principal, generally, may at any time revoke or cancel the agency agreement.
    III. The principal can be held liable to the agent for breach of contract for cancelling the agency agreement without justified grounds.
    IV. The agent may at any time renounce or cancel the agency agreement.
    The CORRECT answer is:

    A. I *only*
    B. I, II
    C. I, III
    D. None of the above

19. Which combination of the following statements is TRUE?
    I. The agency will be automatically terminated by the law upon the happening of any event which makes the agency relationship impractical.
    II. The death of the principal or the agent will automatically cancel the agency relationship.
    III. The death of the principal or the agent will automatically cancel an agency coupled with an interest.
    IV. Knowledge of the death of one party to the agency by the other party is necessary in order for the agency to be terminated.
    The CORRECT answer is:

    A. I, II
    B. I, II, III
    C. I, IV
    D. All of the above

20. Which combination of the following statements is TRUE?
    I. The insanity of either party to the agency generally will automatically terminate the relationship.
    II. Notice to the principal or the agent of the other's insanity is not required.
    III. In the event of the agent's insanity, he may still be able to bind his principal in dealings with third parties who have no knowledge of the insanity or termination.
    IV. The bankruptcy of either party will terminate the agency, except in the case where the bankruptcy has no effect upon the agency or its purpose.

    The CORRECT answer is:

    A. I, III
    B. III, IV
    C. I, III, IV
    D. All of the above

21. Which combination of the following statements is FALSE?
    I. A change of law causing the purpose of the agency to become illegal will cancel the relationship.
    II. An agency to sell liquor in an area which passes a dry law will automatically be terminated.
    III. The destruction or loss of the subject matter of the agency will automatically end the agency.
    IV. The destruction of a house by fire terminates the real estate broker's agency to sell the property.

    The CORRECT answer is:

    A. III only
    B. III, IV
    C. I, III
    D. None of the above

22. Which combination of the following statements is FALSE?
    I. A real estate broker ordinarily is a special agent authorized to conduct a single transaction for his principal.
    II. The broker's principal is always the owner of real property.
    III. The broker's authority is to find a purchaser ready, willing, and able to buy on terms acceptable to the seller.
    IV. The broker may be employed to manage and lease property.

    The CORRECT answer is:

    A. II, IV
    B. IV only
    C. II only
    D. None of the above

23. Which combination of the following statements is TRUE?
    I. A listing is an agreement of employment.
    II. A listing may be oral.
    III. A written listing must be signed by 2 parties.
    IV. If a listing is written, the broker should retain all copies to protect himself.

    The CORRECT answer is:

    A. I, II
    B. I, II, IV
    C. I, II, III
    D. All of the above

24. Which combination of the following statements is FALSE?

    I. A broker who has procured a sale without a prior listing agreement is entitled to compensation.
    II. The law will assist *volunteer* brokers with their claims for compensation to be equitable.
    III. It is difficult for a volunteer broker to collect compensation for a sale.
    IV. The broker cannot collect unless there were words or conduct on the part of the owner from which an agency contract could be implied.

    The CORRECT answer is:

    A. I only   B. I, II   C. III, IV   D. IV only

25. Which combination of the following are types of listing contracts?

    I. Open listing
    II. Exclusive agency
    III. Exclusive listing
    IV. Exclusive right to sell
    V. Multiple listing
    VI. Multiple agency

    The CORRECT answer is:

    A. I, II, IV, V
    B. I, II, IV
    C. I, II, III, V
    D. All of the above

KEY (CORRECT ANSWERS)

1. D
2. D
3. B
4. D
5. B

6. B
7. A
8. C
9. D
10. B

11. A
12. D
13. C
14. B
15. C

16. D
17. D
18. D
19. A
20. D

21. D
22. C
23. C
24. B
25. A

TEST 4

DIRECTIONS: Each question or incomplete statement is followed by several suggested answers or completions. Select the one that BEST answers the question or completes the statement. *PRINT THE LETTER OF THE CORRECT ANSWER IN THE SPACE AT THE RIGHT.*

1. Under an open listing, the owner
    I. will pay a broker commission only on the price listed in the contract
    II. retains the right to list his property with other brokers
    III. must pay a commission to every broker with whom he has listed the property when it has been sold by one of the brokers
    IV. may sell the property himself and save the commission
   The CORRECT answer is:

   A. I, II
   B. II, IV
   C. I, II, III
   D. All of the above

2. Under the exclusive agency listing,
    I. the owner agrees not to list the property with another broker
    II. if the owner sells the property himself, the broker still gets a commission
    III. the broker is more likely to work more diligently than under an open listing
    IV. the owner will not pay a commission to anyone but the listed broker
   The CORRECT answer is:

   A. I, II
   B. II, III, IV
   C. I, III, IV
   D. All of the above

3. Under an *exclusive right to sell listing*,
    I. the broker is given the sole right to sell the property
    II. if the owner should sell the property himself, the owner saves a commission
    III. the broker knows that he will be fully reimbursed for his advertising and soliciting expenses
    IV. the broker is at his best
   The CORRECT answer is:

   A. I, II
   B. I, III, IV
   C. III, IV
   D. All of the above

4. Under a multiple listing,
    I. the broker is given an exclusive right to sell but other brokers may sell the property as sub-agents of the broker
    II. brokers combine through the facilities of a central listing bureau
    III. when the property is sold, the listing broker and the selling broker divide the commission according to the owner-seller's determination
    IV. no specific mention need be made of it in the listing agreement
   The CORRECT answer is:

   A. I, III
   B. I, II
   C. II, III, IV
   D. All of the above

5. A net listing
   I. can occur in connection with an open listing, an exclusive agency listing, an exclusive right to sell listing
   II. is a contract to find a buyer or lessee for the property at a certain net price to the owner
   III. yields the broker as commission any amount over the net price specified to the owner
   IV. is carefully and strictly construed by the courts in light of the broker's duty of loyalty to the owner

   The CORRECT answer is:

   A. I, III
   B. II, III
   C. I, II, III
   D. I, II, IV

6. Net listings
   I. are in widespread popular use in the United States
   II. are frowned upon by the courts, brokers' organizations, and governing bodies
   III. do not usually yield the broker the surplus amount over the net if it appears to be more than the fair commission rate
   IV. do not oblige the owner to restrict his listing to one broker

   The CORRECT answer is:

   A. II, III, IV
   B. I, III, IV
   C. III, IV
   D. II, III

7. Which combination of the following statements is TRUE?
   I. The listing broker may enlist the aid of other brokers to aid him in the sale of the property although no written multiple listing agreement exists.
   II. Cooperative sales agreements may be made between many salesmen who are willing to act as a group.
   III. There is no obligation for the listing broker to accept another broker as his sub-agent.
   IV. Once a listing broker has accepted the aid of another broker, custom will determine how the commission will be divided.

   The CORRECT answer is:

   A. I, II, IV
   B. I, III, IV
   C. III, IV
   D. II, III

8. Which combination of the following statements is FALSE?
   I. It is a violation of his duties as an agent if the broker takes a listing and makes no attempt to sell the property even though the broker feels the owner is asking an unreasonable price.
   II. The broker *sits* on a listing to induce the owner to lower his price.
   III. If a broker is unwilling to work on the listing at the price specified, he should take the listing and try to wear the owner down into lowering his asking price.
   IV. The broker has the duty to follow all reasonable instructions of the owner given in addition to the listing items.

   The CORRECT answer is:

   A. I, III
   B. III *only*
   C. II, IV
   D. None of the above

9. Which combination of the following statements is TRUE?
   I. The broker can lawfully tell a prospective buyer that he knows the seller, his client, will accept an offer of less than the asking price.
   II. The broker should only submit those offers which are within a comprehensible range of the asking price to the owner.
   III. If a client suffers any loss due to the broker's lack of care, knowledge, or skill, he can hold the broker liable for such loss.
   IV. The broker can change the owner's asking price and then submit an offer to his client.

   The CORRECT answer is:

   A. I, II
   B. III *only*
   C. I, III, IV
   D. All of the above

10. Which combination of the following statements is TRUE?
    I. The rate of commission is established by law.
    II. The broker is entitled to a commission if the sale is not consummated due to a defect in the owner's title.
    III. If the buyer wrongfully refuses to complete the sale, the broker receives his commission out of the downpayment forfeited by the purchaser.
    IV. Only the seller may assert a forfeiture.

    The CORRECT answer is:

    A. II, III, IV
    B. I, II, III
    C. II, III
    D. All of the above

11. Which combination of the following statements is FALSE?
    I. If the purchaser makes his offer conditional on some event, then he may rightfully cancel the transaction if the condition does not occur.
    II. If the purchaser cancels a transaction without incurring an obligation, the broker still gets his commission.
    III. If a broker finds a buyer who offers a lower price than that agreed to by the owner in the listing and the owner accepts, the broker is entitled to a commission.
    IV. The buyer usually pays the broker's commission.

    The CORRECT answer is:

    A. I, III
    B. III, IV
    C. II, IV
    D. I, II, IV

12. Agency is essentially that relationship between principal and agents which arises out of a contract wherein the agent is employed to do certain acts in dealing with

    A. other agents
    B. other principals
    C. governmental agencies
    D. third parties

13. The foundation of an agency is an authorization or contract of employment, the terms of which may be either

    A. standardized or customized
    B. written or explicit
    C. long or short
    D. expressed or implied

14. An expressed agreement is an agreement where the terms have been discussed and agreed to by the parties, either

    A. at the beginning or at the end of the term of agreement
    B. verbally or in writing
    C. on a cash or a commission basis
    D. registered or unregistered under the real estate law license

15. An implied contract is one which arises from the act of the

    A. principal   B. agent
    C. real estate license law   D. parties

16. The procuring of signed listings, and preferably exclusive listings, is, in general, _____ by real estate commissions.

    A. encouraged   B. discouraged
    C. tolerated   D. frowned upon

17. In general, verbal contracts of any kind _____ the interests of either the broker or his client.

    A. facilitate   B. enhance
    C. fail to protect   D. satisfy

18. While dual employment will not normally be condoned, a broker may be employed by both the seller and buyer of real estate,

    A. either of whom can avoid payment of compensation
    B. neither of whom can avoid payment of compensation
    C. either of whom can avoid payment of compensation provided that each knew that the broker also represented the other party
    D. neither of whom can avoid payment of compensation provided each knew that the broker also represented the other party

19. It is the duty of the agent of the seller to _____ at the highest price and of the agent for the purchaser to _____.

    A. buy; sell   B. sell; buy
    C. buy; buy   D. sell; sell

20. The law of the place of the contract

    A. is revocable
    B. is irrevocable
    C. is enforceable in accordance with the provisions of the laws of the state in which the land is located
    D. governs its enforcement

21. To entitle a broker to compensation, his services must have been

    A. of a unique character
    B. acknowledged by all parties
    C. the efficient procuring cause of the sale or lease
    D. rendered in accordance with standard operating procedures

22. Which combination of the following statements is TRUE? A broker's compensation is due and payable when
    I. it has been earned
    II. he produces a purchaser who is ready, able, and willing to buy on the seller's terms
    III. he produces a customer who will buy or lease upon the terms specified in the listing
    IV. he brings his client and customer together, and, after mutual bargaining, they come to an agreement, even at a price and on terms materially different from those specified in the authorization

    The CORRECT answer is:

    A. I, II, III   B. II, III, IV
    C. I, III, IV   D. I, II, IV

23. The commission or compensation of a real estate broker is

    A. regulated by statute
    B. legally fixed by the real estate license laws
    C. mutually agreed upon by the broker and his employer
    D. fixed by the real estate board in the community

24. A broker

    A. is legally bound to disclose to his client the identity of a customer
    B. is not legally bound to disclose to his client the identity of a customer
    C. is entitled to his commission where he did not inform his client of the name of a prospective customer and, after the negotiations failed, the purchaser sought out the owner and effected a sale directly
    D. is not entitled to his compensation where the owner refuses to sign a contract of sale on the terms he originally proposed

25. A broker is entitled to his compensation

    A. where, because of some defect, the title to the property is not marketable
    B. although his customer is not ready and able to comply with the terms of the agreement to buy or lease
    C. even if the purchaser is an irresponsible *dummy* and the owner refuses to consummate the transaction
    D. in all of the cases listed above

KEY (CORRECT ANSWERS)

1. B
2. C
3. B
4. B
5. D

6. A
7. B
8. B
9. B
10. A

11. C
12. D
13. D
14. B
15. D

16. A
17. C
18. D
19. B
20. D

21. C
22. D
23. C
24. B
25. A

EXAMINATION SECTION
TEST 1

DIRECTIONS: In continuous discourse, briefly and concisely answer the following questions.

1. What is the position of the real estate broker with reference to the attorneys of the buyers and seller?

    1.____

    ANSWER

    In closing sales and leases, the broker should always recommend the employment of competent legal counsel; many misunderstandings arise out of the doubtless sincere but erroneous advice of these not skilled in the complexities of the law; *home-made* contracts frequently result in trouble and litigation, with a consequent loss to the broker of prestige and good will. The proper fees of the attorneys are paid by the buyer and seller. When the broker fails to recommend legal counsel, he may be injuring not only himself, but those whose interests he is required to protect. A satisfied client is always potentially a *repeat customer* and an asset to any broker.

2. Is it good policy for a broker to give a copy of the listing agreement to the owner who employs him?

    2.____

    ANSWER

    The listing form is a contract and each party to the agreement is entitled to a copy. If the broker's employer is furnished with copies of all listings and other agreements, many future misunderstandings will be avoided. The requirement is that the broker or salesman *shall* give the owner a true, legible carbon copy of the listing.

3. May a real estate salesman be lawfully employed by or accept compensation from any broker other than the broker under whom he is licensed at the time?

    3.____

    ANSWER

    No. Such employment is prohibited by agency law, which in its broadest sense would seem to make any other employment unlawful, referring directly to the so-called *part time* salesman.

4. Where a real estate salesman employed by one broker is assisted in a transaction by a real estate salesman employed by another broker, under an arrangement whereby both salesmen are to have a part of the commission, is it lawful for the first to pay directly to the second salesman the latter's share of the commission?

    4.____

    ANSWER

    No. Payment to the second salesman must be made through his employer broker.

5. Assume that after a listing is taken, and earnest money receipt signed, or a contract executed, a slight change is made in the terms or conditions, and the broker, in the presence of the interested parties, alters the writing to conform to the new arrangement; what precaution should the broker take to protect himself against future misunderstandings?

    5.____

    ANSWER

    Always and without exception, he should have all parties to the contract place their signatures or initials in the margin opposite or nearest the alteration. A better practice is to have the document entirely rewritten.

6. What may a licensed real estate broker lawfully do that a licensed real estate salesman may not do lawfully?

ANSWER

Among other things, a salesman may not transact any phase of the real estate brokerage business in his own name, all must be transacted in the name of the broker by whom he is employed. These phases include: opening and maintaining an office, employing salesmen, listing, advertising, soliciting, negotiating, taking deposits, issuing earnest money receipts, closing transaction, dividing commission, etc.

7. Where a real estate broker who is employed to sell a particular property, buys it himself, but in the name of a *dummy,* will the sale stand if attacked?

ANSWER

No. As agent for the seller, it is the broker's duty to get as much for the property as possible; as buyer, it is to the broker's interest to acquire the property as cheaply as possible; in such a situation there is a direct conflict between duty and self interest; therefore, it is well established that if a broker desires to purchase the property himself, he must before so doing, advise the owner to the effect, if the owner then is willing to proceed, the sale is valid; if the broker does not make a full disclosure, the sale may be set aside. There is nothing inherently wrong in a broker buying his employer's property; the wrong lies in not advising the employer of the broker's true interest in the matter.

8. A broker is employed by an owner to sell a particular property. He introduces a prospective purchaser to the owner, who, a short time later, cancels the contract of employment. Some time later the owner sells to this prospect. Is the broker entitled to his commission?

ANSWER

Yes, in all ordinary cases. The law of agency requires the owner to exercise towards the broker the same good faith as is required of the broker in his dealings with his employer.

9. Is a real estate broker liable in law for frauds and misrepresentations of a salesman working out of his office, where the broker had no knowledge of the misrepresentations and did not participate in them?

ANSWER

Probably yes; if the fraud and misrepresentation were practiced in connection with real estate the broker had for sale.

10. Is a real estate salesman liable to third persons for the misrepresentation of the broker with whom he is associated?

ANSWER

Not unless he participated therein.

11. Why is it necessary that a contract employing a real estate broker to sell real estate for a commission be in writing?

ANSWER

The Statute of Frauds provides that unless such contracts, or some sufficient memo thereof, are in writing, signed by the employer, they are void.

12. How is the Statute of Frauds usually interpreted by the courts? 12.____

    ANSWER
    Strictly against the broker. He has no standing in most courts unless his contract of employment is in writing.

13. What is the position of a broker, who accepts oral employment to sell real estate, and then finds a purchaser who buys the property and pays the owner his full asking price? 13.____

    ANSWER
    In view of the Statute of Frauds, the broker is helpless to recover compensation, wholly irrespective of the fact that the owner has derived a substantial benefit: the law regards the broker as a mere volunteer, offering and giving his services gratuitously. (See the next question for the proper procedure in a similar situation.) Some states are contra, however.

14. Assume that a real estate broker is orally employed to sell real estate; he finds a purchaser to whom he gives a receipt for the earnest money; he then secures the owner's written approval of the sale and the latter's written agreement to pay a commission; is the broker then entitled to his commission? 14.____

    ANSWER
    Yes, provided that the papers sufficiently describe the property, name the parties, the amount of the commission, and either authorize or employ the broker named therein to sell the property, or ratify his employment.

15. What is the difference between a contract giving a broker the exclusive right to sell and a contract giving him an exclusive agency listing with reference to real property? 15.____

    ANSWER
    In a contract for the exclusive right to sell real property, the owner is bound to pay a commission in case of a sale by any person, including himself; while in a contract providing for an exclusive agency listing, the owner merely agrees to employ no other broker in the sale of his property and the owner may sell the property himself without becoming liable for the commission.

TEST 2

DIRECTIONS: In continuous discourse, briefly and concisely answer the following questions.

1. If a husband employs a real estate broker to sell real estate and the broker procures a purchaser ready, able and willing to buy on the husband's exact terms, and the wife then refuses to sign the deed so that the sale is never consummated, is the broker entitled to collect his commission, and if so, from whom?

    ANSWER

    Yes. From the husband.

2. If one employs a broker to sell real estate in which he has no interest whatsoever and the broker finds a purchaser ready, willing and able to buy the real estate on the exact terms and for the exact price stated in the listing contract and then the employer, having no title, is unable to convey, is the broker entitled to his commission?

    ANSWER

    Yes. The broker has fully performed all that he agreed to do and is entitled to the agreed commission.

3. What compensation can a broker recover for services in bringing about a sale of real estate where his contract of employment does not specify the amount thereof?

    ANSWER

    The Statute of Frauds provides in effect that a contract employing a broker to sell real estate must be in writing and if not in writing the contract is void. It occasionally happens that such a contract, though written, fails to specify the amount or rate of compensation to be paid the broker. In some states, the brokerage contract may be enforceable although oral. It is only prudent that, for a broker to recover a commission, for services rendered in connection with the sale of real estate, he should see to it that the amount and the rate of his commission are clearly specified in writing in his contract with his principal; for, if the contract is silent on this point, he may recover nothing, even though his efforts have resulted in the sale of the property, in some states. In other states, however, he can recover the reasonable value of his services. Now, it must be remembered that the final paragraph of an Earnest Money Agreement is a contract between broker and seller, and that extreme care should be used to see that the dollars and cents of commission to be paid is correctly entered.
    In the employment contract, the compensation is shown as a percent of the selling price. In the earnest money agreement the percentage (actual amount) is shown. Do not get carried away and change the 6% of the employment contract to the decimal .06 in the earnest money – you might get just that – 6 cents.

4. Under what circumstances may a broker receive compensation from both parties to the same transaction? Can a broker represent both the seller and purchaser in a sale or exchange of real estate and collect a commission from both?

    ANSWER

    This question has been discussed by the courts upon several occasions and the circumstances outlined under which the broker's double employment is allowable. The rule is that if one employs a broker or accepts his services with knowledge of his employment by another, the written agreement to pay commission can be enforced, if the transaction is otherwise fair and honorable.

The reason for the foregoing rule is based upon the fact that one cannot exercise his whole duty to two principals whose interests are conflicting, it being the duty of the agent for the seller to sell for the highest price and the duty of the agent for the buyer to buy for the lowest price.

5. Where a real estate broker having no written contract for a commission brings about an exchange of properties and the parties to the exchange in their agreement with each other agree to pay a commission, may the broker recover the same?

5.____

ANSWER

No. The law governing the collection of real estate broker's commission requires that every commission contract be in writing, and provides that if the same is not in writing the contract is void and the commission is not collectible. In construing the Statute of Frauds, the courts have repeatedly held that it does not matter how efficient the broker may have been in bringing about a sale or how meritorious the services of the broker may have been, if the agreement to pay a commission is not embodied in writing, signed by the party to be charged, which shows the contracting parties, intelligently identifies the property involved, discloses the terms and conditions of the agreement, and expresses a consideration, the broker is helpless, legally, to collect the promised commission, notwithstanding that he brought about a sale accepted by the owner.

6. Where an owner of real estate authorizes a broker to sell his property at a certain price, and the broker finds a purchaser who pays to the broker a deposit of earnest money to bind the sale, and the owner then refuses to convey, who is liable to the purchaser for the return of the earnest money, the broker or the owner?

6.____

ANSWER

In most of the cases where this question is involved, the broker is found trying to retain the earnest money on the theory that it is due him from the owner as a commission. Though recognizing that the broker has a valid claim against the owner, courts everywhere hold that the broker must look directly to the owner for his compensation, and that he cannot retain the deposit, thus, in effect, forcing the purchaser to pay the owner's debts.

7. What is a sufficient description of real estate in a contract to buy or exchange the same? Must a correct legal description be given, or is it sufficient to refer to the land in general terms?

7.____

ANSWER

A writing concerned with the sale of real property must identify the latter. It is common to say that the writing must describe the property, but the connotation of the word *describe* exacts more than the Statute of Frauds requires. Parol evidence may be used for the purpose of supplying the description to the land, but it is never a valid substitute for missing description. – *In the present instance, no part of the writing gives any indication whatever of the city, county or state in which the property is located; nor does it mention the place where the agreement was effected or the parties reside. As already indicated, no one with the paper in his hand would have any idea where to go in search of the property. In short, a material part of the description is missing and no part of the writing points to the source of evidence aliunde which will identify the property.*

8. Is it correct practice for a salesman to complete a sale and collect in his own name the commission and then give his broker-employer his share of the commission?

8.____

ANSWER
No. The salesman has no right to collect the commission; that right belongs exclusively to his employer; should the salesman receive the commission, he should deliver it immediately to his employer.

9. When earnest money is received by a salesman, is he at liberty to make use of it for his personal account up to the amount of his share of the commission before the deal is closed? If not, what should he do with it?

ANSWER
No. Deposits of earnest money should be delivered by the salesman to his employer immediately; there are no exceptions to this rule.

10. Is it legal for a broker to place a sign on property without the consent of the owner?

ANSWER
No.

11. If a broker is assisted by his grocer in procuring a prospect or in closing a deal, is it lawful for the broker to pay the grocer for his services a fair and reasonable portion of his commission?

ANSWER
No.

12. Is it lawful for a broker to agree with a tenant of the house which the broker has for sale to pay the tenant a portion of the commission should a prospect to whom the tenant shows the property later buy the same?

ANSWER
No.

13. Is it lawful for a broker to pay any third person a stated sum for services rendered in connection with showing the property or assisting in a real estate transaction?

ANSWER
No. Such a payment can not be made whether contingent or otherwise.

14. May a broker's or salesman's license be removed for guaranteeing or promising to a prospective purchaser a definite quick profit on the resale of the property?

ANSWER
No.

15. Does the real estate commissioner have power to compel a broker or salesman to make restitution in cases of fraud and misrepresentation?

ANSWER
No. His sole power is to suspend or revoke licenses.

16. What is meant by *consideration?*

ANSWER
Without being too technical, *consideration* when used with reference to a real estate contract is synonymous with the word *inducement.* Consideration is *that which induces a*

person to act or promise. It is some benefit or advantage to the party promising. Consideration may be money, property, the performance of services or anything else which the law recognizes as having a value.

17. If a broker receives more than one bona fide offer for the same property at approximately the same date, should he select the one to be submitted to the owner?

   17.____

   ANSWER

   No. All bona fide offers, as soon as received, should be submitted to the owner. It is for the owner to determine which offer, if any, should be accepted. The broker should not exercise any discretion in the matter.

18. What is the effect of a deed conveying real estate to husband and wife?

   18.____

   ANSWER

   A deed conveying real estate to a husband and wife creates what is legally known as an *estate by the entireties,* the chief feature of which is the *Tight of survivorship.* If one spouse dies, the surviving spouse takes the whole property free from all claims of the heirs and creditors of the deceased spouse. There is neither dower nor curtesy as to real estate held in the names of husband and wife, as such, agree to purchase real estate will create an estate by the entireties in the properties to be purchased.

19. Where real estate is conveyed to a husband and wife, thus creating an estate by the entireties, and the husband dies, what problem' or other proceedings are necessary before the surviving wife lawfully may sell and convey the prooerty?

   19.____

   ANSWER

   Absolutely none.

20. In a contract for the sale of real estate, John Smith is the purchaser or vendee. He sells his interest to a third person and desires to assign the contract. Is it necessary for his wife to join the assignment?

   20.____

   ANSWER

   Yes, in order to bar a possible dower right.

EXAMINATION SECTION
TEST 1

DIRECTIONS: Each question or incomplete statement is followed by several suggested answers or completions. Select the one that BEST answers the question or completes the statement. *PRINT THE LETTER OF THE CORRECT ANSWER IN THE SPACE AT THE RIGHT.*

1. A contract for the leasing of a piece of real property

   A. must always be in writing
   B. must be in writing if the lease is for more than a year
   C. can be either oral or in writing depending upon the wishes of the parties
   D. never has to be in writing

2. Which of the following is NOT an essential of a valid contract for the sale of real property?

   A. The place, date and hour of closing
   B. Adult parties
   C. The type of mortgage financing
   D. A specification of the form of deed to be delivered

3. It is important to have all covenants agreed upon by the parties expressly provided for in the written contract.
   This is TRUE because

   A. a covenant is not implied in a conveyance of real property
   B. parol evidence is never allowed in a suit on a contract
   C. it is easier to show the intention of the parties later on
   D. a covenant can only be implied if the conveyance contains a special covenant.

4. An incumbrance on the title to real property must be expressed in the contract of sale because it

   A. increases the value of the land
   B. prevents the title to the land from being passed to another
   C. diminishes the value of the land but does not prevent title from being passed
   D. sometimes diminishes, sometimes increases the value of the land, depending upon the type of incumbrance

5. In a contract for the sale of land, which group of the following items MUST be specifically mentioned?
   I. Mortgages on the property
   II. Judgments against the seller
   III. Lis pendens
   IV. Mechanics' liens for work done on the property
   V. The existence of a party wall
   The CORRECT combination is:

   A. I, II, III, IV, V   B. I, II, IV, V
   C. I, II   D. I only

43

6. Which of the following is NOT an incumbrance on the title to land?

    A. An easement across the land
    B. Taxes for local improvements
    C. Restrictive covenants
    D. Zoning regulations

7. A restrictive covenant

    A. can never be enforced in a court of law because it violates Title IV of the Civil Rights Law of 1964
    B. can always be enforced in a court of law
    C. is a limitation on the use of land or other property contained in a deed and may be enforced or not, depending upon the subject of the covenant
    D. enhances the value of the land to the seller since it becomes more exclusive

8. An easement

    A. is a form of covenant
    B. does not have to be specifically detailed in the contract of sale
    C. limits the owner's rights to his own land
    D. none of the above

9. If the phrase, *time is of the essence of this contract,* is incorporated into the body of a real estate contract, it means MOST NEARLY that the

    A. seller must deliver title to the property and the purchaser must make payment on the exact closing date fixed in the contract
    B. exchange of title for purchase price must take place as soon after the closing date as if feasible
    C. contract must be signed within 24 hours after it is drawn up
    D. exchange of title for purchase price must take place within a week of the signing of the contract

10. A and B signed a contract for the sale of A's farm. Incorporated in the contract was the phrase, *time is of the essence of this contract.* The closing date specified in the contract was July 23. On that date, B had the purchase price available to him to make payment to A. A, however, has run into some difficulties regarding his title to the farm and could not present B with good title until July 24. (Nothing regarding the subject property had changed during the delay period.)
    Which of the following statements MOST properly characterizes the situation on July 24?

    A. A and B both have a valid agreement and, since A is now ready to perform, the transaction can be completed.
    B. A had breached the contract by not being prepared on the 23rd with good title and is liable to B for damages.
    C. B is liable to A for damages if he does not go through with the transaction now.
    D. Neither A nor B has to go through with the transaction and no liability rests with either party.

11. The advice of a competent lawyer is

    A. not mandatory where real estate transactions are concerned since a real estate broker is sufficiently capable of handling all matters
    B. not needed where mortgage transactions are concerned since the bank holding the mortgage has its own legal department
    C. advised especially where mortgages are concerned
    D. always needed

12. An action for specific performance is specially suited to real estate transactions for all of the following reasons EXCEPT:

    A. A money judgment for damages is not adequate for land transactions.
    B. It is virtually impossible to find another piece of real estate which is an exact counterpart of the one originally contracted for.
    C. A real estate transaction can be the subject only of a suit in equity.
    D. The best remedy for a real estate suit is to have the contract bargained for signed.

13. A contract for the sale of real property

    A. must always be recorded to be enforced
    B. can never be recorded
    C. can be recorded but does not have to be
    D. must be recorded unless it falls within a section of the Real Property Law

14. One who takes property *subject to* an existing mortgage

    A. assumes payment of the mortgage indebtedness in the event of foreclosure if the property sells for less than the mortgage debt
    B. assume payment of the mortgage indebtedness whether or not the property sells for less than the mortgage debt in the event of foreclosure
    C. becomes the holder of the mortgage
    D. none of the above

15. A sells his house to B who assumes the mortgage thereon. X bank holds the mortgage on the house and forecloses when A does not pay as arranged. X brings an action against B for the full mortgage debt.
    In this action, X will

    A. be successful since B assumed the mortgage debt
    B. fail since he should have brought the action against A
    C. have to sue A and B jointly
    D. be successful against B, and then B can sue A

16. In a transaction for the purchase of land intended for subdivision, the purpose of a *release clause* included in the mortgage is

    A. to enable the purchaser to give clear title to lots in his subdivision
    B. to enable the seller to give clear title to lots in his subdivision
    C. a form of security given to the purchaser by the seller
    D. to release the seller from all promises to the purchaser vis a vis the mortgage

17. A *mortgage subordination clause*

    A. subordinates a contemplated mortgage to secure a loan required to defray the cost of erecting a new building to a mortgage to be taken by the seller as part of the purchase price
    B. subordinates a mortgage to all other loans on the property
    C. subordinates the mortgage to be taken by the seller as part of the purchase price to a contemplated mortgage to secure a loan to alter a building
    D. none of the above

18. Which combination of the following statements is TRUE?
    I. Legal descriptions of property are not required in a lease.
    II. Rezoning residence lots into business lots always increases their value.
    III. Taxes become a lien against real property on January 1st.
    IV. An option for which no consideration is given is not enforceable.

    The CORRECT combination is:

    A. I, II
    B. I, III, IV
    C. III, IV
    D. I, II, III, IV

19. Which combination of the following statements is TRUE?
    I. Building restrictions as shown in a deed are not encumbrances.
    II. Trees, shrubs, and vines are real property while in the ground.
    III. The amount of money to be deposited with an *offer to buy* is fixed by law.
    IV. Quit claim deed may convey fee title to real estate.

    The CORRECT combination is:

    A. I, II, III
    B. I, II, IV
    C. II, III
    D. II, IV

20. Which combination of the following statements is FALSE?
    I. A city lot 49' X 187' contains 8163 sq. ft. of land.
    II. Zoning laws are local regulations to beautify cities.
    III. Restrictions are limitations upon the use of property by deed or law.
    IV. The rights of a party in possession need not be considered in negotiating the sale of real property.

    The CORRECT combination is:

    A. I, II, IV
    B. I, II, III
    C. II, III
    D. III, IV

21. Which combination of the following statements is TRUE?
    I. As soon as the grantor signs the deed and has acknowledged it, title passes to the grantee.
    II. The earnest money receipt is one of the most important (if not the most important) instruments in a real estate transaction.
    III. Personal property may become real property when it is permanently attached to the land.
    IV. A lease is a contract.

    The CORRECT combination is:

    A. I, II, IV
    B. III, IV
    C. IV only
    D. II, III, IV

22. Which combination of the following statements is TRUE?
    I. An estate is an interest which one has in property.
    II. A written contract for land supersedes a verbal contract.
    III. The market value of a home is the cost of the lot, plus the present day replacement cost of the building thereon.
    IV. The Statute of Frauds requires all contracts to be in writing.
    The CORRECT combination is:

    A. I, II
    B. II only
    C. IV only
    D. I, II, IV

23. Which combination of the following statements is FALSE?
    I. Specific performance is a court action to compel performance of a contract.
    II. The term *encumbrance* includes any legal claim against property.
    III. A mortgage is given as security for a debt.
    IV. A contract is an agreement expressed or implied to do or not to do a certain thing.
    The CORRECT combination is:

    A. I, IV
    B. II, IV
    C. II, III
    D. None of the above

24. Which of the following statements concerning the term *valuable consideration* as it pertains to a real estate broker, are CORRECT?
    I. *Valuable consideration* must be only money consideration.
    II. *Valuable consideration* may be in the form of property.
    III. *Valuable consideration* may consist of the rendition of services.
    IV. *Valuable consideration* may be in the granting of a favor.
    V. Even slight value will be enough to constitute *valuable consideration*.
    The CORRECT combination is:

    A. I only
    B. I, II
    C. II, III, IV, V
    D. II, III, IV

25. Which combination of the following statements is FALSE?
    I. To own a fee simple is to be an absolute owner.
    II. An appraisal is an estimate of quality, quantity, or value.
    III. To amortize is to extinguish a debt.
    IV. Taxes are charges levied by a political subdivision to obtain revenue for carrying on the functions of the government.
    The CORRECT combination is:

    A. III only
    B. I, III
    C. II, IV
    D. None of the above

KEY (CORRECT ANSWERS)

1.	B	11.	C
2.	C	12.	C
3.	A	13.	C
4.	C	14.	D
5.	A	15.	A
6.	D	16.	A
7.	C	17.	C
8.	C	18.	B
9.	A	19.	D
10.	B	20.	A

21. D
22. A
23. D
24. C
25. D

TEST 2

DIRECTIONS: Each question or incomplete statement is followed by several suggested answers or completions. Select the one that BEST answers the question or completes the statement. *PRINT THE LETTER OF THE CORRECT ANSWER IN THE SPACE AT THE RIGHT.*

1. Which combination of the following statements is TRUE?
    I. Assessments are charges levied by a political subdivision to collect revenue for some improvement made in a given area against the property which is benefited by such improvement.
    II. In a chattel mortgage, the title to the property is transferred to the buyer immediately on his promise to pay.
    III. In a conditional sales contract, the title to the property remains with the seller until all the payments of the property are paid in full.
    IV. A chattel is personal property, such as household goods, automobiles, money, and personal effects.
   The CORRECT combination is:

   A. I, IV
   C. I, III
   B. All of the above
   D. II, IV

2. Which combination of the following statements is FALSE?
    I. There is no difference between an easement and a license.
    II. An attorney-in-fact is anyone appointed by the landowner to handle his property for him.
    III. If the buyer defaults on his payment to the seller of property he may retrieve the earnest money he put down as a deposit.
    IV. A land contract provides for execution of a deed when all installments have been paid, or when the unpaid balance of the purchase price has been reduced to a certain agreed amount, whereupon the buyer is to receive a deed and give the seller a mortgage or note for the balance of the purchase price.
   The CORRECT combination is:

   A. I only
   C. III, IV
   B. I, III
   D. None of the above

3. Which combination of the following statements is TRUE?
    I. An option is simply a contract by which a landowner gives another person the right to buy the land at a fixed price within a specified time.
    II. A judgment is the determination of the legal rights of any party against another.
    III. Constructive notice is never a legal substitute for actual knowledge.
    IV. Zoning ordinances are exercises of the police power of the municipality.
   The CORRECT combination is:

   A. I, II   B. I, II, IV   C. I, II   D. I, II, III

49

4. Which combination of the following statements is TRUE?
   I. An encumbrance is any legal claim against property which is recognized by law.
   II. A prospect is anyone who has a need or desire for a piece of property and who has the money or credit to buy it.
   III. A lease is a written contract.
   IV. A covenant is a promise.
   The CORRECT combination is:

   A. I only
   B. I, II, III, IV
   C. I, II
   D. I, III, IV

5. Which combination of the following statements is FALSE?
   I. 840 sq. ft. is an acre
   II. An agent represents a principal in dealing with third parties.
   III. A bill of sale transfers personal property.
   IV. Consideration is a term used to denote something of value.
   The CORRECT combination is:

   A. I only
   B. I, III
   C. III, IV
   D. I, IV

6. Which combination of the following statements is TRUE?
   I. A deficiency judgment is a judgment for the balance owing after the security given has been collected and applied on the principal owing.
   II. An encumbrance is a right or interest in a piece of real estate; this interest will prohibit the owner from issuing a deed subject to it.
   III. Foreclosure is the sale of property by legal proceeding to sell any rights or interest which a mortgagor had when he entered into the mortgage.
   IV. To grant is to give possession of property to another by written deed.
   The CORRECT combination is:

   A. I, II, IV
   B. I, III, IV
   C. II, III, IV
   D. I, II, III, IV

7. Which combination of the following statements is FALSE?
   I. A homestead is a certain amount by which the home and property occupied by an owner is protected by law from attachment and sale for the claims of creditors.
   II. A paper or document which gives the holder certain legal claims and rights is valid even when it is unsigned.
   III. *Obsolete* means out-of-date
   IV. Restrictions limit the use of property.
   The CORRECT combination is:

   A. II only
   B. I, II
   C. I, III
   D. II, III

8. Which combination of the following statements is TRUE?
    I. A zoning ordinance is a ruling passed by the police department limiting the use of property, e.g., in respect to the heights of buildings, building areas, etc.
    II. A chattel is personal property.
    III. The statute of frauds requires that contracts for land be in writing, signed by the owner or his agent.
    IV. Clear title to a home cannot be conveyed unless both husband and wife sign listings and the contract of sale.

    The CORRECT combination is:

    A. I, II, III, IV
    B. II, III, IV
    C. I, II, III
    D. I, II, IV

9. Which combination of the following statements is FALSE?
    I. An escrow is a safe depository for funds and documents until the conditions of the transaction are fulfilled.
    II. An easement is the privilege granted by an owner of land to another to use his land for a particular purpose.
    III. The owner's equity is what his share in the property is worth after claims such as mortgages and liens are discharged.
    IV. Real estate transactions are escrowed for the protection of both the buyer and seller.

    The CORRECT combination is:

    A. I only
    B. IV only
    C. III, IV
    D. None of the above

10. Which combination of the following statements is TRUE?
    I. If no time is specified in the contract, the buyer is entitled to possession upon delivery of the deed.
    II. The seller is permitted to remove shrubs and flowers after he has signed to sell his house as long as the buyer has not taken possession.
    III. A prospective purchaser may withdraw his offer and demand the return of his deposit before the seller has accepted it.
    IV. Land includes everything on, below, and above the surface of the earth.

    The CORRECT combination is:

    A. I, II
    B. I, II, III
    C. II, III
    D. I, III, IV

11. Which of the following are rights enjoyed under the American system of ownership?
    I. Possession
    II. Control
    III. Enjoyment
    IV. Disposition

    The CORRECT combination is:

    A. I, II, IV
    B. I, II
    C. II, IV
    D. I, II, III, IV

12. The rights enjoyed under the American System of ownership are
    I. not limited
    II. limited by the power of eminent domain
    III. limited by the police power
    IV. limited by taxation
    V. limited by escheat
    The CORRECT combination is:

    A. I only   B. II, III   C. II, III, IV, V   D. II, IV

13. Which combination of the following statements is FALSE?
    I. *Pro rata* means to bring up-to-date all pending pecuniary assets affecting the property as to the date of the transfer of title.
    II. Taxes, rents, insurance, interest on mortgages are some examples of things that are pro rated.
    III. A fixture is an object so attached to the property that if it were removed it would cause considerable damage to the property.
    IV. Real estate may be considered as land and the attachments thereto.
    The CORRECT combination is:

    A. I, IV   B. I, II
    C. I only   D. None of the above

14. Which of the following is an accurate description of a *lessee*?

    A. Seller   B. Lender
    C. One who holds the lease   D. One who owns the lease

15. Which of the following is an accurate description of a *lessor*?

    A. One who holds the lease   B. Borrower
    C. One who owns the lease   D. Seller

16. Which of the following is an accurate description of a *grantor*?

    A. Lender   B. Borrower   C. Seller   D. Buyer

17. Which of the following is an accurate description of a *grantee*?

    A. Lender   B. Borrower   C. Seller   D. Buyer

18. Which of the following is an accurate description of a *Mortgagor*?

    A. Lender   B. Borrower   C. Seller   D. Buyer

19. Which of the following is an accurate description of a *Mortgagee*?

    A. Lender   B. Borrower   C. Seller   D. Buyer

20. Which of the following are rights reserved by the state to restrict land ownership?
    I. Eminent domain
    II. Police power
    III. Taxation
    IV. Escheat
    The CORRECT combination is:

    A. I, IV   B. II, IV   C. II, III   D. I, II, III, IV

21. Information collected by the real property inventory can be used to advantage in the real estate business by

    A. the listing of vacancies in given areas
    B. the listings of the depreciation of property in given areas and the causes which brought them about
    C. the listing of the population trends in given areas
    D. all of the above

22. Which of the following is a type of *property description* used in describing a parcel of real estate?

    A. Street and address
    B. Metes and bounds
    C. Monuments
    D. All of the above

23. Which of the following is the PRINCIPAL type of co-ownership of property?

    A. Tenancy in common
    B. Joint tenancy
    C. Tenancy in entirety
    D. All of the above

24. Upon a buyer's default under a sales contract when the down payment has been made and before title is closed, which of the following is the appropriate course of action for the seller to follow?

    A. Sue for breach of contract
    B. Demand the contract to become void
    C. Retain the down payment or earnest money
    D. All of the above

25. Which combination of the following statements is FALSE?
    I. A legatee is an heir or recipient of property, real or personal, by will.
    II. Real property is permanent in nature and is immobile.
    III. Personal property is mobile.
    IV. Zoning restricts the types that can be used for residential, business, and industrial purposes.

    The CORRECT combination is:

    A. I, III
    B. IV only
    C. II, III
    D. None of the above

KEY (CORRECT ANSWERS)

1.	B	11.	D
2.	B	12.	C
3.	B	13.	C
4.	B	14.	C
5.	A	15.	C
6.	B	16.	C
7.	A	17.	D
8.	B	18.	B
9.	D	19.	A
10.	D	20.	D

21. D
22. D
23. D
24. D
25. D

TEST 3

DIRECTIONS: Each question or incomplete statement is followed by several suggested answers or completions. Select the one that BEST answers the question or completes the statement. *PRINT THE LETTER OF THE CORRECT ANSWER IN THE SPACE AT THE RIGHT.*

1. The deposit of a buyer is given

   A. as part payment of the purchase price
   B. to cover escrow expenses
   C. to assure the broker and salesman of a commission
   D. to be forfeited if the deal fails

2. To alienate property, one

   A. advertises it for sale
   B. sells it to a foreigner
   C. conveys title
   D. uses it for payment of judgment in a suit of alienation of affections

3. The legal rights which a wife possesses upon the death of her husband in lands owned by him in fee simple, are called

   A. curtesy
   B. share by the entirety
   C. dower
   D. share in common

4. The title to land held in absolute ownership is called

   A. a leasehold
   B. record title
   C. fee simple
   D. ownership in common

5. The FIRST instrument a buyer usually signs in a real estate transaction is a(n)

   A. mortgage
   B. deed
   C. bill of sale
   D. offer to purchase

6. The interest on $75,000 for four months at 5 1/2% per annum is

   A. $2,501.00   B. $1,375.00   C. $1,956.00   D. $2,253.00

7. The state of ownership of real property where the undivided interest of two or more owners is with survivorship, is known as

   A. estate by the entirety
   B. estate in joint tenancy
   C. estate in common
   D. an undivided interest estate

8. When a person has an interest in land which is to continue as long as he lives, he is said to have a(n)

   A. estate for years
   B. easement
   C. life estate
   D. dower right

9. An absolute, basic requirement of a simple contract is

   A. acknowledgment by a notary public
   B. an official recording
   C. offer and acceptance
   D. a monetary consideration

10. An option WITHOUT valid consideration is

    A. valid   B. unenforceable   C. void   D. binding

11. The tax on a given piece of property is determined by multiplying the tax rate by the

    A. value of the property
    B. insured value
    C. assessed valuation of the property
    D. market value of the property

12. The landlord is called the

    A. devisee   B. lessor   C. mortgagor   D. trustee

13. An option contract differs from a contract of sale in that the

    A. option need not be consummated
    B. option needs no consideration
    C. contract of sale is enforceable on either party to it
    D. contract of sale requires consideration

14. A FUNDAMENTAL requirement of a contract is

    A. offer and acceptance
    B. acknowledgment by a notary public
    C. recordation at the court house
    D. use of the proper printed form

15. A percentage lease is USUALLY based on a percentage of the

    A. assessed value of the property
    B. gross sales of the business
    C. tenant's net worth
    D. market value of the property

16. Severalty ownership of real estate

    A. denotes ownership by several persons
    B. demonstrates that there are several ways to own real estate
    C. represents sole ownership by a single person
    D. results from a severance in condemnation proceedings

17. In offsetting depreciation, one may

    A. combine functional and economic obsolescence
    B. use the sinking fund or the straight line method
    C. include the plottage value
    D. lower the rate of contemplated capitalization of the net income

18. Federally chartered savings and loan associations are regulated by the   18.____

    A. Federal Reserve Bank
    B. Building and Loan Commissioner
    C. Federal Home Loan Bank Board
    D. Corporation Commissioner

19. The MAXIMUM amount guaranteed by the government on a SBA loan is   19.____

    A. 65% of the value of the property
    B. 90%; 50% on first mortgage; 40% on second
    C. without limit on rental units
    D. the same as FHA

20. Leases on agricultural lands may run   20.____

    A. not more than 20 years   B. a maximum of 99 years
    C. no more than 51 years   D. no limit

21. Involuntary alienation of an estate means that   21.____

    A. the estate cannot be transferred without the consent of the owner
    B. aliens are forbidden to own estates in fee simple
    C. ownership of estates may be transferred by operation of law
    D. no one can be compelled to transfer title without his consent

22. Escheat is a legal term meaning that   22.____

    A. a fraud has been committed
    B. property has reverted to the State
    C. an agent's license has been revoked
    D. property under a trust deed may be reconveyed

23. A contract of sale passes   23.____

    A. the full fee simple title to the purchaser
    B. only an equitable title
    C. the legal title
    D. an estate for years

24. First-half taxes become delinquent on real property on   24.____

    A. the first Monday in March
    B. July 1st
    C. December 10 at 5 p.m.
    D. the first Monday in May

25. A married woman is legally capable of contracting at the MINIMUM age of   25.____

    A. seventeen   B. eighteen
    C. twenty   D. twenty-one

KEY (CORRECT ANSWERS)

1.	A	11.	C
2.	C	12.	B
3.	C	13.	A
4.	C	14.	A
5.	D	15.	B
6.	B	16.	C
7.	B	17.	B
8.	C	18.	C
9.	C	19.	B
10.	C	20.	C

21.	C
22.	B
23.	C
24.	C
25.	B

TEST 4

DIRECTIONS: Each question or incomplete statement is followed by several suggested answers or completions. Select the one that BEST answers the question or completes the statement. *PRINT THE LETTER OF THE CORRECT ANSWER IN THE SPACE AT THE RIGHT.*

1. How much would a salesman receive if he splits with his broker an 8% commission on a $100,000 sale?

    A. $2,000   B. $4,000   C. $6,000   D. $8,000

2. The MINIMUM time which must run after publication of a notice to creditors, under the provisions of the Uniform Commercial Code (UCC) pertaining to bulk sales, before consummation of the sale, is _____ days.

    A. 5   B. 10   C. 15   D. 20

3. As a result of the sale of a home, $1,600 was charged by a lender for *discount points*. The buyer obtained a maximum FHA loan. All details of the sale were processed through escrow.
   The payment of the points would be provided for by a(n)

    A. deduction from the principal amount of the loan to the buyer
    B. deduction from the amount due the seller
    C. addition to the principal amount of the buyer's loan
    D. deduction from the buyer's down payment

4. To be valid, a bill of sale MUST be

    A. dated   B. signed
    C. notarized   D. witnessed

5. Property held in joint tenancy, upon the death of one of the tenants, passes to the

    A. landlord   B. state
    C. county assessor   D. surviving joint tenant

6. Alienation expresses a meaning most completely OPPOSITE to

    A. acquisition   B. ad valorem
    C. acceleration   D. amortization

7. Anything that is fastened or attached to real property permanently is considered to be _____ property.

    A. personal   B. real
    C. private   D. separate

8. In the appraisal of residential property, the cost approach is MOST appropriate in the case of _____ property.

    A. new   B. middle-aged
    C. older   D. multi-family

9. The instrument used to secure a loan on personal property is called a

   A. bill of sale
   B. trust deed
   C. security agreement
   D. bill of exchange

10. A promissory note that provides for payment of interest ONLY during the term of the note is a(n) _____ note.

    A. installment
    B. straight
    C. amortized
    D. non-negotiable

11. Community property is property owned by

    A. churches
    B. husband and wife
    C. the municipality
    D. the community

12. A property produced an 8% gross return on a $100,000 purchase price for a one-year period. The owner's only expense resulted from a 6% annual interest charge on a $90,000 lien against the property.
    What is the percentage of return the owner is realizing on his equity?

    A. 8%   B. 10%   C. 12%   D. 26%

13. The seller is sometimes called the

    A. vendee   B. vendor   C. lessee   D. lessor

14. Which of the following is the BEST example of functional obsolescence?

    A. Rotten mud sill
    B. Massive cornices in an apartment building
    C. Decline of the neighborhood
    D. Adverse zoning across the street from subject property

15. A financing statement may be released from the records by

    A. payment in full
    B. a reconveyance
    C. filing a release statement
    D. death of the mortgagor

16. An owner-operator, who has $20,000 invested in a business, receives $7,100 annual earnings (including his salary) from the business.
    Allowing him $450 per month as salary, the financial return on his investment is

    A. 5 1/2%   B. 6 1/3%   C. 8%   D. 8.5%

17. The interest rate for a *conventional* loan secured by a first trust deed is USUALLY

    A. the same as for a FHA loan
    B. more than for a FHA loan
    C. the same no matter what the source of the funds
    D. the maximum rate allowed by law

18. A contract based on an illegal consideration is

    A. valid
    B. void
    C. voidable
    D. enforceable

19. A business encumbered by a $3,000 security agreement on the fixtures, was sold for $18,000.
    At 7 1.2% the broker's commission was

    A. $135   B. $1,125   C. $1,350   D. $1,500

20. The stock and fixtures that are to be transferred with the sale of a business are USUALLY enumerated in a(n)

    A. contract of sale   B. inventory
    C. deed   D. appraisal

21. A check that has been altered or raised by a person other than the maker is

    A. valid   B. invalid
    C. cancelled   D. dishonorable

22. A valid bill of sale MUST contain

    A. a date   B. an acknowledgment
    C. the seller's signature   D. a verification

23. The rate of commission to be charged for selling a business is determined by

    A. the real estate commissioner
    B. agreement between seller and broker
    C. agreement between buyer and broker
    D. state law

24. Of the following, the item considered personal property is

    A. installed fencing   B. growing trees
    C. a trust deed   D. an installed water heater

25. A security agreement is USUALLY given in connection with

    A. real property   B. agricultural property
    C. rentals   D. personal property

KEY (CORRECT ANSWERS)

1. B
2. A
3. B
4. B
5. D

6. A
7. B
8. A
9. C
10. B

11. B
12. D
13. B
14. B
15. A

16. D
17. B
18. B
19. B
20. B

21. B
22. C
23. B
24. C
25. D

EXAMINATION SECTION
TEST 1

DIRECTIONS: Each question consists of a statement. You are to indicate whether the statement is TRUE (T) or FALSE (F). *PRINT THE LETTER OF THE CORRECT ANSWER IN THE SPACE AT THE RIGHT.*

1. A mortgage is a conveyance of a security interest in land, to secure payment of a debt. 1.____

2. When the mortgage note is made payable *to the order of* the creditor, it is *negotiable,* and even though the debtor may have a defense against the mortgagee, he will NOT be able to use this defense against a third person who bought the note and mortgage in good faith and got it endorsed before it was due. 2.____

3. A *cognovit* clause permits the taking of a judgment on the note WITHOUT suit in court. 3.____

4. If the defaulting debtor does NOT pay by the time agreed, he loses all right to the land. 4.____

5. Creditors can eliminate the debtor's equity of redemption by putting such a clause in the mortgage. 5.____

6. The debtor-mortgagor has a right to pay up late, which continues until it is cut off by an approved foreclosure sale or until he voluntarily deeds it away. 6.____

7. If the debtor-mortgagor defaults, an acceleration clause in the mortgage, or perhaps in the note, can be relied upon to declare the whole balance due. 7.____

8. After a default, if the mortgagee and mortgagor CANNOT agree on a voluntary close-out, the only way the mortgagee can kill off the equity of redemption is through foreclosure by sale. 8.____

9. After a foreclosure sale, the mortgagee CANNOT in the future go against the mortgagor for the deficiency. 9.____

10. A purchase money mortgage is an ordinary mortgage given to secure purchase money for the land put up as a security. 10.____

11. A purchase money mortgage may be given to the seller or it nay be given by the buyer to a third person who lends part of the purchase price to the buyer. 11.____

12. A wife's dower claims are junior to the rights of the holder of a purchase money mortgage. 12.____

13. A judgment lien on the property prior in time to a purchase money mortgage is superior to it. 13.____

14. If a person gives a mortgage on one piece of land to raise money to buy another piece, this is a purchase money mortgage. 14.____

15. When a purchaser of real estate on which there exists a mortgage, takes the land and assumes to pay the mortgage, the original mortgagor (the seller) is released from all personal liability under the mortgage. 15.____

16. A mortgagee can get a deficiency judgment against a *non-assuming* buyer. 16.____

63

17. A mortgagee can sell the note and mortgage to a third party who becomes the assignee   17.___
    of the mortgage claim, and the assignee has EXACTLY the same rights and remedies
    the mortgagee had,

18. It is wise for the assignee to give notice of the assignment in writing to the mortgagor,   18.___
    directing the mortgagor to make all further payments to the assignee instead of the mort-
    gagee.

19. The assignee as a holder in due course of a negotiable note, takes free of mortgagor's   19.___
    defenses like misrepresentation, failure of consideration, and others, even though they
    are available against the mortgagee.

20. It is NOT important for the assignment of the mortgage to be recorded.   20.___

21. In the case of a mortgage, the total amount of the mortgage indebtedness need NOT be   21.___
    stated as the consideration, you can use the *one dollar and other good and valuable con-
    sideration* formula used in filling out deed forms.

22. The mortgage to be recordable MUST be executed with the same formalities as a deed.   22.___

23. Revenue stamps are required for a mortgage.   23.___

24. The mortgagee-creditor MUST sign the mortgage for it to be valid.   24.___

25. The recording fee for a mortgage is paid by the mortgagee.   25.___

KEY (CORRECT ANSWERS)

1. T	11. T
2. T	12. T
3. T	13. F
4. F	14. F
5. F	15. F
6. T	16. F
7. T	17. T
8. T	18. T
9. F	19. T
10. T	20. F

21. F
22. T
23. F
24. F
25. F

TEST 2

DIRECTIONS: Each question consists of a statement. You are to indicate whether the statement is TRUE (T) or FALSE (F). *PRINT THE LETTER OF THE CORRECT ANSWER IN THE SPACE AT THE RIGHT.*

1. A mortgage is a pledge of property as security for a debt.   1.___

2. A mortgage is actually comprised of two writings - a promissory note and the mortgage document.   2.___

3. If the mortgage contains an acceleration clause and the note does not, the provisions of the note control.   3.___

4. The note given in a mortgage is a negotiable instrument.   4.___

5. A mortgage is a contract and to be valid MUST contain all the elements of a contract.   5.___

6. The mortgagor is the lender.   6.___

7. When personal property is the security, the instruments are identified as a real property mortgage.   7.___

8. A mortgage is treated as a lien against the property with the title vesting in the mortgagee.   8.___

9. The priority of the lien is created by the time of its recording.   9.___

10. Under the *title theory,* the mortgagor passes title to the mortgagee and, upon payment of the debt, the title reverts to the mortgagor.   10.___

11. Usually, all improvements are a part of the mortgaged property and are subject to the mortgage lien.   11.___

12. When the mortgagor fails to pay taxes, assessments, interest on prior mortgages, insurance premiums, or other charges necessary for the protection of the lien, the mortgagee may pay any or all of the costs and add the amount to the mortgage debt.   12.___

13. Mortgages may NOT be assigned.   13.___

14. Real property mortgages are USUALLY one of three classes - FHA insured mortgage, GI guaranteed mortgage, and the conventional mortgage.   14.___

15. An amortizing mortgage retires the debt by a series of equal monthly payments of both principal and interest.   15.___

16. A straight mortgage calls for the payment of interest ONLY during the term of the note.   16.___

17. A deficiency judgment is USUALLY sought in a mortgage foreclosure when the sales does not bring a sufficient amount to satisfy the debt.   17.___

18. As a general rule, all governmental liens become a first lien on the property.   18.___

19. A purchase money mortgage can take precedence over a government lien.   19.___

20. A trust deed involves three parties: the grantor, the trustee, and the beneficiary. 20.____

21. The note which is secured by the trust deed is given by the grantor to the trustee. 21.____

22. The trustee and the beneficiary may be the same person. 22.____

23. The PRINCIPAL difference between a trust deed and a mortgage is in the method of foreclosure. 23.____

24. If a mortgagee is obligated to make advances to the extent of a sum stated in the mortgage, the lien of the mortgage is security for all such advances, whether made before or after notice of subsequent encumbrances. 24.____

25. If the title to the real property upon which the mortgage or trust deed is a lien is conveyed to someone else, such conveyance changes the obligation of the original maker of the note. 25.____

KEY (CORRECT ANSWERS)

1.	T	11.	T
2.	T	12.	T
3.	F	13.	F
4.	T	14.	T
5.	T	15.	T
6.	F	16.	T
7.	F	17.	T
8.	F	18.	T
9.	T	19.	F
10.	T	20.	T

21. F
22. F
23. T
24. T
25. F

TEST 3

DIRECTIONS: Each question consists of a statement. You are to indicate whether the statement is TRUE (T) or FALSE (F). *PRINT THE LETTER OF THE CORRECT ANSWER IN THE SPACE AT THE RIGHT.*

1. An agreement between the seller and buyer to the effect that the buyer will assume and pay the obligation will have the effect of subjecting the purchaser to personal liability for the debt.

2. If NOT expressly stated in the deed to assume the mortgage, the mere fact that the purchaser continues to pay, or seeks an extension of the loan, will, in itself, subject the purchaser to personal liability.

3. A deed which *excepts* a lien of a mortgage or trust deed will NOT result in the assumption of personal liability.

4. A deed which says *subject to a mortgage which grantee assumes and agrees to pay* will result in the assumption of the obligation.

5. If a purchaser should enter into an extension agreement with the holder of the mortgage to extend the obligation for another period, the extension agreement will relieve the original maker from liability unless he consents to the extension.

6. A water bill is a lien against the real property and can be enforced against the premises.

7. A title search before purchase will reveal the existence of a delinquent water bill.

8. An encumbrance is anything which affects or limits the fee simple title to the property.

9. The lien created by a mortgage is an equitable lien.

10. Encumbrances GENERALLY restrict or impair the owner's powers to convey the property subject to the encumbrances.

11. A tax lien is an involuntary lien.

12. Assessments are distinguished from general taxes in that general taxes are presumed to benefit all property within the taxing district equally, whereas the special assessments are levied ONLY on particular pieces of property because of the peculiar benefit that the assessed property may derive from the contemplated improvement.

13. In the event that the property owner fails to make payment of the amounts due either with respect to the ad valorem taxes or special assessments for local improvements, the law permits the levying body, county or city, as the case may be, to institute a suit to foreclose the lien of such tax or assessment and cause the property to be sold to satisfy the obligation.

14. If the owner of the property fails to redeem after foreclosure within the time provided, he will USUALLY be granted an extension of the redemption period if the purchaser at the foreclosure sale is a unit of the government.

15. Any person or firm supplying material or labor for the construction, improvement, alteration, or repair of real property or structures thereon, shall be entitled to a lien against that property to secure payment of the money due him for such material or services supplied.   15.____

16. A mechanic's lien would include a lien on materials and labor used in the construction of portable fixtures moved onto the premises and NOT attached to the property.   16.____

17. A mortgage is a voluntary lien.   17.____

18. The part of the mortgage designated as a promissory note is a negotiable instrument and may be assigned.   18.____

19. It is necessary that the mortgage be properly acknowledged by the mortgagors before a notary public in order that the mortgage may be recorded so as to impart constructive notice to third persons dealing with the land.   19.____

20. A mechanic's lien is an inchoate lien.   20.____

21. The Federal Tax Lien Act restores the priority of all obligations secured by a mortgage over federal tax liens filed after the mortgage is executed and recorded.   21.____

22. Parties whose claims are adverse or superior to that of the mortgagor at the time of the foreclosure sale are NOT affected by the decree.   22.____

23. If the indebtedness is NOT paid when due and foreclosure by the mortgagee results, the original mortgagor, but not any subsequent owners of the property who have assumed and agreed to pay the debt, may be held personally liable in the event that a sale of the property does not produce sufficient funds to discharge the entire balance owing on the mortgage, including interest and costs of foreclosure.   23.____

24. USUALLY title insurance will exclude from coverage claims arising out of material or labor liens.   24.____

25. It is important that the buyer inspect the property prior to purchase in order to be aware of any repairs, alterations, or remodeling work that is being done which may give rise to a mechanic's lien.   25.____

KEY (CORRECT ANSWERS)

1.	T	11.	T
2.	F	12.	T
3.	T	13.	T
4.	T	14.	F
5.	T	15.	T
6.	F	16.	F
7.	F	17.	T
8.	T	18.	T
9.	T	19.	T
10.	F	20.	T

21. T
22. T
23. F
24. T
25. T

———

TEST 4

DIRECTIONS: Each question consists of a statement. You are to indicate whether the statement is TRUE (T) or FALSE (F). *PRINT THE LETTER OF THE CORRECT ANSWER IN THE SPACE AT THE RIGHT.*

1. A broker or salesman SHOULD have at least rudimentary knowledge about the legal nature of a mortgage, as well as know how to fill out mortgage notes and mortgage forms as such.
   1.____

2. There is ONLY one kind of mortgage note, which is uniform throughout the states.
   2.____

3. The negotiable *order* form of mortgage note is popular because the debtor will have a defense even against a third person who bought the note and mortgage in good faith and got it endorsed before it was due.
   3.____

4. Some mortgage notes contain so-called *cognovit* clauses which permit the taking of judgment on the note by bringing suit in court.
   4.____

5. Few creditors are content to take mortgage notes WITHOUT *cognovit* clauses.
   5.____

6. In the so-called *lien theory* states, the mortgage grants to the creditor a mere mortgagee's *lien* on the land to secure the debt. The debtor retains legal title and with it the right to possess and to use the land.
   6.____

7. The right on the part of the defaulting debtor-mortgagor to pay up late, as long as he pays interest for the period of the delay, is called the mortgagor's equity of redemption.
   7.____

8. The MOST effective method of limiting the equity of redemption is through provisos in the mortgage itself.
   8.____

9. In closing out a defaulted mortgage on a voluntary out-of-court basis, the creditor enjoys virtually a free hand.
   9.____

10. A mortgagor who is behind in his payments no longer has the power to transfer what he owns.
    10.____

11. One of the MOST effective ways of avoiding the expense and problems of foreclosing a mortgagor's equity of redemption is to require the debtor to deliver, in form, an out-and-out deed, instead of a mortgage, to the creditor.
    11.____

12. If the parties cannot agree, the ONLY way the mortgagee can kill off the equity of redemption is through foreclosure by sale.
    12.____

13. In the *purchase money mortgage,* the security rights of the seller or of the third person lender are protected against outside claims.
    13.____

14. An example of a purchase money mortgage is the situation in which a person gives a mortgage on one piece of land to raise money to buy another piece.
    14.____

15. It is good practice to indicate on purchase money mortgages that *this is a purchase money mortgage,*
    15.____

16. The so-called trust deed mortgage is the USUAL form of mortgage in some states.
    16.____

17. It is illegal for the buyer of mortgaged property to refuse to assume the mortgage debt. 17.___

18. When the mortgagee sells the note and mortgage to a third party, this person who is called the *mortgagor* steps into the mortgagee's shoes. 18.___

19. The name of the debtor-mortgagor SHOULD appear in the mortgage exactly as it appears in the deed by which he took title. 19.___

20. If the mortgagor is a married man, his wife MUST join in order to make her dower interest superior to the mortgage lien. 20.___

21. Do NOT use the wife's given first name and initial, like *Sally P. Smith,* but rather *Mrs. Charles R. Smith.* 21.___

22. If the mortgagor is a married woman, and her husband does NOT own any interest in the land as joint tenant or tenant in common, then he need not sign. 22.___

23. The husband MUST be named and MUST sign in the case where his wife's real estate is their homestead. 23.___

24. A mortgagee does NOT sign the mortgage. 24.___

25. The mortgagee customarily pays the attorney fee for drafting the mortgage. 25.___

KEY (CORRECT ANSWERS)

1. T	11. F
2. F	12. T
3. F	13. T
4. F	14. F
5. F	15. T
6. T	16. T
7. T	17. F
8. F	18. F
9. F	19. T
10. F	20. F

21. F
22. T
23. T
24. T
25. F

TEST 5

DIRECTIONS: Each question consists of a statement. You are to indicate whether the statement is TRUE (T) or FALSE (F). *PRINT THE LETTER OF THE CORRECT ANSWER IN THE SPACE AT THE RIGHT.*

1. Use the *One Dollar ($1.00) and other good and valuable consideration* formula in filling out deed forms. 1._____

2. Use the same care and accuracy in describing real estate in a mortgage which you would use in a deed. 2._____

3. Revenue stamps are required for a mortgage. 3._____

4. The mortgagor-creditor does NOT sign the mortgage. 4._____

5. A mortgage is commonly defined as a pledge of property as security for a credit. 5._____

6. *Mortgage* ACTUALLY designates two writings or documents the promissory note and the mortgage document itself. 6._____

7. The two instruments, note and mortgage, are to be construed together. 7._____

8. If, however, there is a conflict between the note and the mortgage with respect to maturity of the debt, the provisions of the mortgage control. 8._____

9. If the mortgage contains an acceleration clause and the note does NOT, the provisions of the note control. 9._____

10. The note given in a mortgage is an example of a negotiable instrument, an indispensable factor in commerce like the common bank check. 10._____

11. The *holder in due course* provision of state law does NOT establish any protections for the third party in the transfer of negotiable instruments. 11._____

12. A mortgage in which real property is pledged to secure a debt is USUALLY referred to as a *chattel mortgage*. 12._____

13. The *lien law theory* treats a mortgage as a lien against the property, the title remaining with the mortgagee. 13._____

14. A majority of the states follow the *title theory* as opposed to the *lien law theory*. 14._____

15. Under the title theory, the mortgagee passes title to the mortgagor. Upon payment of the debt, the title reverts to the mortgagee. 15._____

16. Under the lien law theory, a mortgage of real property is a conveyance so as to enable the owner of the mortgage to recover possession of the property WITHOUT a foreclosure and sale. 16._____

17. The MOST popular form of mortgage, one highly developed by the FHA, is the amortizing mortgage which retires the debt by a series of equal monthly payments of both principal and interest. 17._____

18. Real property mortgages are USUALLY one of three classes FHA insured mortgage, GI guaranteed mortgage, and the conventional mortgage. 18.___

19. The purchase money mortgage is MERELY an extension of credit by the buyer to the seller. 19.___

20. As a general rule, all governmental liens become a second lien on the property. 20.___

21. Legal requirements applying to chattel mortgages are found in the Uniform Commercial Code. 21.___

22. Trust deeds are given to secure loans on real estate and perform the same function as a real estate mortgage. 22.___

23. A mortgage involves three parties, the trust deed two parties. 23.___

24. The trustee and the beneficiary MUST be two different persons or corporations and CANNOT be the same, since the purpose of the trust deed is to have an individual or company other than the lender or borrower control the security. 24.___

25. In filling out a trust deed, the property owner and his wife will be named as *Beneficiary* a title insurance company or one of the other eligible parties would be named as *Grantor* and the lender (whether an individual, mortgage company, bank, or savings and loan association) would be named as *Trustee*. 25.___

KEY (CORRECT ANSWERS)

1.	F		11.	F
2.	T		12.	F
3.	F		13.	F
4.	T		14.	F
5.	F		15.	F
6.	T		16.	F
7.	T		17.	T
8.	F		18.	T
9.	F		19.	F
10.	T		20.	F

21.	T
22.	T
23.	F
24.	T
25.	F

EXAMINATION SECTION
TEST 1

DIRECTIONS: Each question consists of a statement. You are to indicate whether the statement is TRUE (T) or FALSE (F). *PRINT THE LETTER OF THE CORRECT ANSWER IN THE SPACE AT THE RIGHT.*

1. The names of the grantor (seller) and the grantee (buyer) MUST appear on the deed, and it is a good policy also to show their addresses

1.____

2. It is NOT important to make the spouse of the grantor a party to the deed.

2.____

3. If the spouse of a married grantor is made a party to a deed, then the spouse of the grantor will still have a dower or courtesy right in the real estate conveyed.

3.____

4. The words of conveyance state clearly what the instrument purports to accomplish.

4.____

5. If the purpose of the instrument is to quitclaim, then the words, *"Grant, Bargain and Sell, and Convey"* could be used.

5.____

6. The words generally in use in warranty deeds that accomplish the desired result are, *"Release, Remise, Convey and Quitclaim."*

6.____

7. For a deed, any description that clearly identifies the property to be conveyed is sufficient.

7.____

8. The deed MUST be signed or executed by the grantor.

8.____

9. The object of the acknowledgment is to admit an instrument to record legally and to be able to produce it in evidence WITHOUT other proof of execution.

9.____

10. The acknowledge of a deed SHOULD be made before a notary public or other officer permitted to take acknowledgments on deeds in the state.

10.____

11. In general warranty deed, the grantor, in addition to granting the property, covenants with the grantee, his heirs and assigns, that he will warrant and defend such property for the grantee, his heirs, personal representatives and assigns against the claims and demands of all persons whomsoever.

11.____

12. From the point of view of the grantee, the quitclaim deed is the safest kind of deed he can secure.

12.____

13. In a special warranty deed, the grantor warrants ONLY against acts of the grantor himself and all persons claiming by, through and under him.

13.____

14. A quitclaim deed conveys that interest, whatever it may be, which the grantor has in the real property and with no statement of warranty.

14.____

15. The entire burden and risk is on the grantor in the case of a quitclaim deed.

15.____

16. Under a quitclaim deed the grantor and his personal representatives, his heirs or assigns will ALWAYS have a right to challenge or make demands upon the land, and the use of such deed warrants that other parties might have a claim to the land and the grantee accepts the property subject to this risk.

16.____

17. A deed of trust is a deed in which the title to the property is conveyed to a third person, called a trustee, who holds the property in trust to secure payment of a debt described in the instrument. 17.____

18. With a trust deed, the grantor (borrower) retains possession, use and control of the property. 18.____

19. After the indebtedness which was secured by the deed of trust has been paid off, the trustee or noteholder effectuates a release of the deed of trust. 19.____

20. With a deed of trust, in the event of default by the grantor of the debt, the trustee, after advertising the property for sale, sells the property and credits the grantor with the proceeds of the sale. 20.____

21. When a grantor conveys his property to a trustee to secure a debt, the trustee MUST pay all taxes, keep the improvements in tenantable condition and commit no waste. 21.____

22. A foreclosure of a mortgage can ONLY be accomplished through court action. 22.____

23. Mortgages and deeds of trust do NOT have to be recorded. 23.____

24. A mortgage is a conditional conveyance of the real estate upon which the loan is made directly to the mortgagee (lender) from the mortgagor (borrower). 24.____

25. A deed is operative when SIGNED by both parties. 25.____

KEY (CORRECT ANSWERS)

1.	T	11.	T
2.	F	12.	F
3.	F	13.	T
4.	T	14.	T
5.	F	15.	F
6.	F	16.	F
7.	T	17.	T
8.	T	18.	T
9.	T	19.	T
10.	T	20.	T
21.	F		
22.	T		
23.	F		
24.	T		
25.	F		

TEST 2

DIRECTIONS: Each question consists of a statement. You are to indicate whether the statement is TRUE (T) or FALSE (F). *PRINT THE LETTER OF THE CORRECT ANSWER IN THE SPACE AT THE RIGHT.*

1. The title to any parcel of real estate is contained in and controlled by the recorded and filed documents in the public records of the state in which the land is situated. 1.____

2. Under provisions of the recording acts, the public has constructive notice of all property recorded and of all filed papers. 2.____

3. Abstracting is the *briefing* or *digesting* of the particular records affecting a given parcel of land. 3.____

4. It is not necessary for the abstract to show that a lien exists on the particular property. 4.____

5. It is possible for a person to have a good abstract and at the same time have very poor title. 5.____

6. An abstract can cover hazards such as missing heirs and forged deeds. 6.____

7. The title insurance policy is an insured statement of the condition of the title. 7.____

8. A title insurance policy will insure against an unrecorded easement for public utility purposes. 8.____

9. Mining claims and water rights can be ascertained by searching the county records. 9.____

10. Adverse possession by a squatter will not be insured against by a policy of title insurance. 10.____

11. Zoning ordinances are taken into consideration by a policy of title insurance. 11.____

12. Title insurance is the opinion of the ownership and marketability of title to a particular parcel of real property. 12.____

13. Title insurance indemnifies the insured in the event of a loss by reason of a defect or a flaw in title prior to the date of the policy. 13.____

14. A title plan is a private collection of public records meeting the minimum rules of the state's title insurance laws. 14.____

15. The primary source of the escrow agent's duties and responsibilities is the written instructions of the parties. 15.____

16. One of the essential functions of the escrow agent is to assemble the necessary data from which the required financial adjustments between the parties can be made. 16.____

17. The general purport of recording statutes is to permit, rather than to require, the recordation of any instrument which affects the title to or possession of real property, and to penalize the person who fails to take advantage of the privilege of recording. 17.____

18. As between conflicting claims to the same parcel of land, priority of recordation will ordinarily determine the rights of the parties. 18.____

19. The effect of recording an instrument is to give implicit notice to all the world of the content of any instrument or document filed for record. 19.___

20. Mere recording does NOT validate a void or defective instrument. 20.___

21. The courts have ruled that the benefits of a recording statute are available to one who takes title with ACTUAL notice of a previously executed though unrecorded instrument. 21.___

22. It has been ruled that POSSESSION of land by a person other than the record owner is constructive notice to the purchaser (or to the person acquiring an interest in or liens upon said property from such owner) of the right, title, interest or claim of the possessor. 22.___

23. Since recording is not compulsory, A, an unscrupulous owner of record, might first sell a given parcel of land to B, who takes possession but doesn't record, and then sell the same parcel to C, who carelessly relies solely on the records showing A as owner. Title would remain in A despite the innocent, good faith payment by C. 23.___

24. A deed of trust MUST be executed and recorded subsequent to commencement of any work at all in order to assure its priority. 24.___

25. Tax and assessment liens generally prevail over private real property interests. 25.___

KEY (CORRECT ANSWERS)

1.	F	11.	F
2.	T	12.	T
3.	T	13.	F
4.	F	14.	T
5.	T	15.	T
6.	F	16.	T
7.	T	17.	T
8.	F	18.	T
9.	F	19.	F
10.	T	20.	T

21.	F
22.	T
23.	F
24.	F
25.	T

TEST 3

DIRECTIONS: Each question consists of a statement. You are to indicate whether the statement is TRUE (T) or FALSE (F). *PRINT THE LETTER OF THE CORRECT ANSWER IN THE SPACE AT THE RIGHT.*

1. The quitclaim deed does NOT convey, nor does it purport to transfer the property only the right, title and interest, if any, in the property.   1.____

2. The quitclaim deed is USUALLY used as a release.   2.____

3. The quitclaim deed contains MOST of the covenants of warranty although it does not contain all of them.   3.____

4. The quitclaim deed does NOT have the protection of the recording acts as against a prior unrecorded conveyance.   4.____

5. The quitclaim deed can safely be used for passing title.   5.____

6. Title insurance companies will insure on a quitclaim deed.   6.____

7. The quitclaim deed is accepted as being *prima facie* evidence that it will accomplish a full and complete conveyance of title.   7.____

8. If the grantor has previously conveyed the title to another, by any form of deed, the grantee in such deed will take title even though the subsequent quitclaim deed is recorded first.   8.____

9. By accepting the quitclaim deed the grantee has been put on notice that someone else may have the prior right to the title.   9.____

10. The grantee who accepts a quitclaim deed is classed as a bona fide purchaser.   10.____

11. The covenant of seizin in a warranty deed assures the grantee that the grantor has the estate in quantity and quality that he purports to convey and he covenants that the premises are free from encumbrances.   11.____

12. The special warranty deed limits the warranty to only those acts or deeds committed by the grantor.   12.____

13. Modern methods of insuring titles have alleviated the absolute necessity of insisting upon a warranty deed.   13.____

14. In a well-prepared warranty deed the covenants of title and warranty are made subject to all existing liens and encumbrances.   14.____

15. It is NOT necessary that spouses join in every conveyance of real property.   15.____

16. The ONLY important instance in which husbands and wives need not sign a deed is in the case of a partnership where dower and curtesy do not attach.   16.____

17. A transfer of real property to husband and wife USUALLY creates a tenancy by the entirety.   17.____

18. A deed WITHOUT a date is valid.   18.____

19. The word *delivery* as it pertains to a deed is universally understood to be the physical act of handing over. 19._____

20. If a spouse is adjudged insane by a court having jurisdiction, and is committed to a public insane asylum, during the continuance of such disability the other spouse may convey any real estate owned in his or her sole right and acquired after the other spouse has been committed to the insane asylum, in the same manner as though they had never been married. 20._____

21. Consideration includes the amount of cash and any lien, mortgage, contract, or other encumbrance existing against the property and agreed to be paid or assumed by the purchaser. 21._____

22. Under the escrow method of closing, title insurance companies accept all the necessary documents to a transaction, check title records, examine the instrument, and see to the recording. 22._____

23. The buyer pays the recording fee for his deed, and the fee for any mortgage he himself puts on the property. 23._____

24. Leasehold interests CANNOT be recorded. 24._____

25. The acknowledgment of the deed before a notary public validates the deed. 25._____

KEY (CORRECT ANSWERS)

1.	T	11.	T
2.	T	12.	T
3.	F	13.	T
4.	T	14.	T
5.	F	15.	F
6.	F	16.	T
7.	F	17.	T
8.	T	18.	T
9.	T	19.	T
10.	F	20.	T

21. T
22. T
23. T
24. F
25. F

TEST 4

DIRECTIONS: Each question consists of a statement. You are to indicate whether the statement is TRUE (T) or FALSE (F). *PRINT THE LETTER OF THE CORRECT ANSWER IN THE SPACE AT THE RIGHT.*

1. Deeds customarily are signed ONLY by the purchaser. 1.____

2. The buyer of real estate is called the grantee. 2.____

3. The purpose of the deed is to convey the described interest in real estate from the buyer to the seller. 3.____

4. USUALLY a deed conveys fee simple ownership. 4.____

5. A deed may NOT be used to convey a land contract buyer's interest in mortgaged land. 5.____

6. USUALLY the seller delivers a warranty deed to the buyer. 6.____

7. In a warranty deed, the seller guarantees that his title is free and clear of all encumbrances EXCEPT those expressly mentioned in the deed. 7.____

8. The warranty in a warranty deed NOT only guarantees the seller's ownership but also guarantees the building that may be located on the land. 8.____

9. The grantor in a quitclaim deed MERELY conveys what title he has, if any. 9.____

10. A quitclaim deed is USUALLY used to clear up flaws in title. 10.____

11. Revenue stamp requirements arise from Federal excise tax. 11.____

12. A deed to a purely fictitious person is void, but a deed to an actual person under a fictitious name by which he is known or which he assumes for the occasion is valid. 12.____

13. Mortgages, taxes, or assessments which are liens on the property before the deed and which are NOT removed as a part of the sale deal are not deductible when computing the revenue stamps requirements. 13.____

14. A deduction is permitted for any lien or encumbrance placed on the property in connection with the sale. 14.____

15. The buyer USUALLY pays for the revenue stamps. 15.____

16. An escrow is essentially a small and short-lived trust arrangement. 16.____

17. If revenue stamps in the required amount are NOT fixed to the deed, the deed is invalid. 17.____

18. Frequently, the stamps as shown in the public records are consulted for the purpose of finding out what the previous buyer paid for the land. 18.____

19. As soon after execution as practicable, the deed SHOULD be recorded by the seller in the office of the register of deeds in the county in which the land described is located. 19.____

20. The seller USUALLY pays the recording fee, while the buyer USUALLY pays the attorney's fee if the deed was drafted by a lawyer. 20.____

21. A deed to a fictitious person is valid.

22. A deed to an actual person under an assumed name is binding.

23. A grantee MUST sign the deed?

24. If there is more than one grantee, it will be necessary to designate whether they take as joint tenants or as tenants in common.

25. If the grantees are husband and wife, they will by law take as joint tenants UNLESS tenancy in common is expressly indicated.

KEY (CORRECT ANSWERS)

1.	F	11.	T
2.	T	12.	T
3.	F	13.	F
4.	T	14.	F
5.	F	15.	F
6.	T	16.	T
7.	T	17.	F
8.	F	18.	T
9.	T	19.	F
10.	T	20.	F

21. F
22. T
23. F
24. T
25. T

EXAMINATION SECTION
TEST 1

DIRECTIONS: Each question consists of a statement. You are to indicate whether the statement is TRUE (T) or FALSE (F). *PRINT THE LETTER OF THE CORRECT ANSWER IN THE SPACE AT THE RIGHT.*

1. A broker is employed to sell a parcel of property for which he is to receive a set fee as a commission. Without informing the seller, he also acts for the purchaser who is also to pay a commission.
   The seller discovers this and refuses to pay any commission.

   The broker is entitled to the commission. 1.____

2. A listing to sell or rent property and obtain a fixed specified price for the owner is a net listing. 2.____

3. A real estate broker holding a sixty-day exclusive agency to sell a parcel of real property may not collect a commission if he sold the property to his wife without disclosing such relationship. 3.____

4. A broker is entitled to his commission if he produces a buyer ready, willing and able to meet the terms proposed by the seller in his listing even if the owner refuses to go through with the deal. 4.____

5. An owner lists his property with a broker for $60,000. The broker finds a purchaser ready to pay the $60,000, but the broker and the purchaser enter an agreement that if the property can be obtained for $55,000, the two would divide the $5,000 saved.
   The seller agrees to sell for $55,000.

   The broker is still entitled to a commission. 5.____

6. There is an *implied* covenant in every lease that the premises are fit for the use for which they are intended. 6.____

7. A demising clause is an essential part of every lease. 7.____

8. A landlord has the right to send mechanics into leased premises to make alterations even though the lease contains no specific authority to do so. 8.____

9. A tenant who assigns his lease to a third party is relieved of the responsibility he originally assumed. 9.____

10. A lease on a property being sold constitutes an encumbrance on that property. 10.____

11. Wayne leases a building to Hart for a period of five years at an annual rental of $30,000. At the expiration of the five-year period Hart remains in possession.

    Under these conditions, the lease is automatically renewed for a period of one year. 11.____

12. A contract by which the owner agrees with another person that he shall have a right to buy the property at a fixed price within a certain time is called a binder. 12.____

13. In order to protect his commission, it is advisable for a broker to draw up the contract of sale.   13.___

14. No covenant is implied in a contract for the sale of real property.   14.___

15. When a house is destroyed by fire after an agreement of sale is signed, the loss falls upon the purchaser.   15.___

16. A written binder is executed for the sale of a parcel of real property. Before the date of the signing of the contract, the property is partially destroyed by fire.   16.___

    The purchaser may refuse to complete the transaction even if the seller restores the property.

17. In the sale of a private dwelling, a gas range in the kitchen is not considered to be a fixture and may be removed on the sale of the property.   17.___

18. A means of acquiring title where the occupant has been in actual, open, notorious, exclusive and continuous occupancy of property under a claim of right is called *adverse possession*.   18.___

19. A person appointed by a court to manage the estate of a person who dies *intestate* is called an *administrator*.   19.___

20. A *covenant of seizin* is a referee's guarantee that the property was seized by an order of the court for the nonpayment of a mortgage.   20.___

21. In an action for specific performance, the court will *always* compel the seller to deliver a full covenant and warranty deed.   21.___

22. Property of a person who dies intestate, leaving no heirs, passes to the state by the law of *eminent domain*.   22.___

23. An acknowledgment is unnecessary in a bond.   23.___

24. In the purchase of real property, it is generally more advisable to assume the payment of an existing mortgage, rather than to buy the property subject to the existing mortgage.   24.___

25. A mortgage with amortization provisions therein is offered for sale two years after its inception.   25.___
    In order to effect a proper and sound transfer the purchaser of said mortgage should receive an assignment plus a mortgage reduction certificate.

KEY (CORRECT ANSWERS)

1. F
2. T
3. T
4. T
5. F

6. T
7. T
8. F
9. F
10. T

11. T
12. F
13. F
14. F
15. F

16. T
17. F
18. T
19. T
20. F

21. F
22. F
23. T
24. F
25. F

TEST 2

DIRECTIONS: Each question consists of a statement. You are to indicate whether the statement is TRUE (T) or FALSE (F). *PRINT THE LETTER OF THE CORRECT ANSWER IN THE SPACE AT THE RIGHT.*

1. In order to safeguard his interests, the mortgagee should have the mortgage duly recorded. 1.___

2. When a purchaser of property assumes an existing mortgage, the original mortgagor is not relieved of his obligations under the mortgage. 2.___

3. The mortgage covenant which permits the mortgagee to advance the due date of the principal of the mortgage is called the *acceleration clause*. 3.___

4. An individual who evaluates real property for the purpose of determining the amount of taxes to be charged against the property is called an *appraiser*. 4.___

5. Unpaid taxes are *usually* considered to be attachments. 5.___

6. A receiver in foreclosure does NOT require a license as a real estate broker. 6.___

7. A person employed by a real estate broker whose only duly is to collect rentals from several buildings, does NOT require a license as a real estate salesman. 7.___

8. A broker who knows that misrepresentations are being made by his salesman is not subject to disciplinary action if he, himself, does not make these misrepresentations. 8.___

9. The real estate licensing board does NOT assume jurisdiction over complaints arising out of controversies over commissions. 9.___

10. A real estate salesman may accept listings of real property and may advertise real property for sale *only* in the name of his employing broker. 10.___

11. A minor may obtain a salesman's license. 11.___

12. A non-citizen may become a broker. 12.___

13. A salesman may sell real estate without a license. 13.___

14. A salesman must take an examination. 14.___

15. A licensed broker must exhibit a sign. 15.___

16. A broker may collect a commission if he has no license at the time of contract, but obtains one prior to title closing. 16.___

17. A person engaged in real estate management need NOT have a license. 17.___

18. A person who buys and sells real estate on his own account is NOT required to have a license. 18.___

19. A janitor who merely collects rents must have a license. 19.___

20. One who obtains *listings* and distributes them to brokers for a fee does NOT need a license.   20.____

21. A part-time salesman does NOT need a license.   21.____

22. A business broker who sells real estate in connection with the sale of a business does NOT need a broker's license.   22.____

23. One who sells a lease for another is required to be licensed.   23.____

24. A person employed to negotiate a mortgage loan for another is NOT required to have a license.   24.____

25. Violation of the licensing law is a crime.   25.____

KEY (CORRECT ANSWERS)

1.	T		11.	T
2.	T		12.	T
3.	T		13.	T
4.	F		14.	T
5.	F		15.	T
6.	T		16.	T
7.	F		17.	F
8.	F		18.	F
9.	T		19.	F
10.	T		20.	F

21. F
22. T
23. T
24. F
25. T

EXAMINATION SECTION
TEST 1

DIRECTIONS: Each question or incomplete statement is followed by several suggested answers or completions. Select the one that BEST answers the question or completes the statement. *PRINT THE LETTER OF THE CORRECT ANSWER IN THE SPACE AT THE RIGHT.*

1. A real estate broker is the holder of a sixty-day *exclusive agency* for the sale of a parcel of real property.
   The broker, with only one-half of his exclusive agency expired, should

   A. claim one-half of the commission from the estate
   B. continue his efforts to sell for the balance of his agreement
   C. refer to the owner's death in his advertising
   D. discontinue his efforts to sell

2. An example of a fiduciary relationship is that which exists between a broker and

   A. a financing company
   B. his client
   C. the real estate licensing division
   D. his salesman

3. A broker may NOT collect a commission from both the buyer and the seller *without*

   A. an exclusive right to sell
   B. notifying both after the sale is made
   C. an exclusive agency
   D. prior consent of both buyer and seller

4. Fox has the right to sign Wolf's name to a contract for the sale of real property.
   He (Fox)

   A. is a special agent
   B. is an optionee
   C. has a power of attorney
   D. is an attorney at law

5. A broker who brings about the meeting of the minds of the buyer and the seller is said to be the

   A. exclusive agent   B. fiduciary agent
   C. procuring cause   D. grantee

6. A real estate broker's license was suspended but he continued to do business. He negotiated the sale of a parcel of real property and, upon completion of his services, made a claim for the commission earned.
   Under these circumstances, the commission is payable to

   A. the courts   B. the broker
   C. the purchaser   D. no one

7. The deed which a purchaser *usually* receives at a foreclosure sale is a(n) _____ deed.

   A. bargain and sale
   B. quit claim
   C. referee's
   D. administrator's

8. Ownership of property transfers when the

   A. deed is executed
   B. contract is signed
   C. deed is delivered
   D. deed is recorded

9. The title to land held in absolute ownership is called a(n)

   A. estate for years
   B. leasehold
   C. fee simple
   D. base fee

10. Escrows are created for the protection of the

    A. property
    B. buyer and seller
    C. broker
    D. escrow holder

11. Property limited to a specific use or purpose designated by a governmental authority is said to be

    A. designed   B. coded   C. condemned   D. zoned

12. Title to fixtures, shelves, counters, and merchandise is transferred by

    A. the deed
    B. a bill of sale
    C. a chattel mortgage
    D. escrow

13. The person to whom the title to real property is conveyed is called the

    A. grantor   B. devisee   C. grantee   D. executor

14. For what reason are deeds recorded?

    A. To insure title
    B. To give notice to the world
    C. It is required by the state
    D. To save the cost of title insurance

15. An item of personal property may be called

    A. a freehold
    B. realty
    C. tenure
    D. a chattel

16. The purchaser at a foreclosure action receives a(n) _____ deed.

    A. quit claim
    B. bargain and sale
    C. executor's
    D. referee's

17. A deed becomes effective when it has been

    A. acknowledged
    B. delivered
    C. signed
    D. recorded

18. A deed is a

    A. bond
    B. conveyance
    C. freehold
    D. mortgage

19. To be enforceable, a lease of real property must be in writing, if it is for a period of *more than*

    A. 30 days
    B. 60 days
    C. 90 days
    D. one year

20. A lease of property whereby the lessor is to meet all property charges regularly incurred through ownership is called a(n) _____ lease.

    A. gross
    B. assigned
    C. percentage
    D. net

21. If a lease does not specify when rent is to be paid, it is payable _____ month.

    A. on the first of each
    B. in the middle of the
    C. any day in the
    D. on the last day of the

22. The person who borrows the money and pledges his property as security is known as the

    A. mortgagee
    B. assignor
    C. grantor
    D. mortgagor

23. A mortgage which is taken back as part of the selling price is called a(n) _____ mortgage.

    A. subordinated
    B. amortizing
    C. blanket
    D. purchase money

24. In order to induce a would-be purchaser to complete a transaction, a broker offers to divide his commission with him. Upon completion of the transaction, the broker refuses to give the purchaser any part of the commission.
    The broker would be required to give the purchaser _____ of the commission.

    A. one-half
    B. no part
    C. one-fourth
    D. one-third

25. An example of an agency relationship is that which exists between a broker and

    A. a financing company
    B. his salesmen
    C. the real estate licensing division
    D. the National Association of Realtors

KEY (CORRECT ANSWERS)

1.	D	11.	D
2.	B	12.	B
3.	D	13.	C
4.	C	14.	B
5.	C	15.	D
6.	D	16.	D
7.	C	17.	B
8.	C	18.	B
9.	C	19.	D
10.	B	20.	A

21. D
22. D
23. D
24. B
25. B

TEST 2

DIRECTIONS: Each question or incomplete statement is followed by several suggested answers or completions. Select the one that BEST answers the question or completes the statement. *PRINT THE LETTER OF THE CORRECT ANSWER IN THE SPACE AT THE RIGHT.*

1. A written listing of property for sale with a real estate broker is an

   A. expressed agreement of employment
   B. implied agreement of employment
   C. exclusive agency
   D. exclusive right to sell

2. A limitation placed upon the use of property is called a

   A. *lis pendens*   B. violation
   C. restriction   D. lien

3. X and Y sign a binder for the sale of a parcel of real property, with the provision that a formal contract would be signed the next day. The following day, X refused to go through with the deal.
   Y can sue for

   A. foreclosure   B. breach of warranty
   C. fraud   D. specific performance

4. A deed which removes a cloud from the title of real property is called a

   A. special warranty deed   B. quit claim deed
   C. deed of confirmation   D. release deed

5. According to prevailing custom, and unless otherwise expressed, revenue stamps must be purchased and attached to the deed by the

   A. broker   B. purchaser   C. mortgagee   D. seller

6. Under the Statute of Frauds, a lease of real property must be in writing if it is written for a period in excess of

   A. 30 days   B. 60 days   C. 90 days   D. one year

7. When a commercial property is being offered for sale, and a tenant wishes to renew a long-term lease, the managing broker should renew the lease with a(n) _____ clause.

   A. percentage   B. cancellation
   C. distraining   D. elevator

8. An instrument that creates a lien on real estate to secure the repayment of a loan is called a

   A. bond   B. deed   C. mortgage   D. lease

9. An instrument executed by the mortgagee setting forth the balance due on the mortgage as of the date of the execution of the instrument is called a(n)

   A. estoppel certificate
   B. amortization agreement
   C. mortgage reduction certificate
   D. prepayment agreement

10. The law which governs the relationship between a real estate broker and his client is

    A. Contract Law
    B. the Statute of Frauds
    C. the Real Property Law
    D. the Law of Agency

11. The usual and customary rates of commission paid for the brokerage of real estate are those suggested by

    A. the real estate licensing division
    B. the state legislature
    C. local real estate boards
    D. local courts

12. Two competing brokers claim the commission on the negotiation of a real estate transaction.
    It is paid to the broker

    A. making the first claim for commission
    B. who first introduced the parties
    C. who was the procuring cause
    D. with whom the property was first listed

13. A lease of property which requires the lessor to pay *all* property charges incurred through ownership is called a _____ lease.

    A. gross   B. net
    C. ground   D. percentage

14. The termination of a lease when caused by some act or omission on the part of the landlord, which act or omission prevents the tenant from occupying the property for the purpose designated in the lease, is called

    A. surrender and acceptance
    B. destruction of property
    C. constructive eviction
    D. actual eviction

15. B and S sign a contract for the sale of a parcel of real property, with the provision that the property will be turned over the next day.
    The following day S refuses to go through with the deal.
    B can sue for

    A. foreclosure   B. breach of warranty
    C. fraud   D. specific performance

16. Any right to or interest in real property that diminishes its value is called an

    A. estoppel B. amortization agreement
    C. abstract D. encumbrance

17. The GREATEST interest one may have in real estate is called a(n)

    A. life tenancy B. fee simple
    C. hereditament D. fiduciary

18. Title to real estate passes at the time the deed is

    A. recorded B. delivered
    C. signed D. acknowledged

19. A clause found in a blanket mortgage which gives the owner of the property the privilege of paying off a portion of the mortgage indebtedness, thus freeing a portion of the property from the mortgage lien, is called a(n) _____ clause.

    A. prepayment B. release
    C. subordination D. amortization

20. The person who lends the money and to whom the property is mortgaged is known as the

    A. mortgagee B. assignor C. grantee D. mortgagor

21. Under a *net* rental agreement, the tenant generally pays all but which one of the following?

    A. Taxes B. Assessments
    C. Fire insurance D. Interest on mortgage

22. A real estate broker drew a lease providing that the rent was to be paid monthly, but did not specify therein that the rent should be paid in advance.
    In such a case, the rent is due and payable

    A. on the first of the month
    B. on the 15th day of the month
    C. on the last day of the month
    D. any day in the month upon demand

23. A lease on real estate is an instrument which

    A. transfers title
    B. places a lien on real estate
    C. transfers possession
    D. secures the repayment of a loan

24. The wearing away of land through processes of nature, as by a stream or by the wind, is called

    A. escheat B. erosion
    C. depreciation D. obsolescence

25. A broker's written binder signed by the seller to sell homestead property at a price to a buyer is enforceable by the   25.___

    A. broker in an action for commission
    B. buyer in an action to close title
    C. seller in an action against the buyer for damages for failure to close
    D. is no force and effect

KEY (CORRECT ANSWERS)

1.	A	11.	C
2.	C	12.	C
3.	B	13.	B
4.	B	14.	C
5.	D	15.	D
6.	D	16.	D
7.	B	17.	B
8.	C	18.	B
9.	C	19.	B
10.	D	20.	A

21.	D
22.	C
23.	C
24.	B
25.	A

EXAMINATION SECTION
TEST 1

DIRECTIONS: Each question or incomplete statement is followed by several suggested answers or completions. Select the one that BEST answers the question or completes the statement. *PRINT THE LETTER OF THE CORRECT ANSWER IN THE SPACE AT THE RIGHT.*

1. A lease for more than one year must be

    A. recorded
    B. acknowledged
    C. in writing
    D. delivered

2. Money given on a binder is called

    A. an option
    B. earnest money
    C. an escrow
    D. a listing

3. The broker refuses commission. The salesman may sue

    A. the broker
    B. the seller
    C. the broker and the seller
    D. no one

4. Who does NOT need a real estate license?

    A. A lawyer who hires salesmen
    B. One who sells listings
    C. An auctioneer of real estate
    D. A referee in a foreclosure

5. In the foreclosure of a tax lien, the buyer receives a(n)

    A. bargain and sale deed
    B. full covenant and warranty deed
    C. referee's deed
    D. administrator's deed

6. A salesman discontinues his employment with a broker. He must

    A. obtain his broker's consent
    B. notify the real estate licensing board
    C. return his license
    D. do nothing

7. A violation of the real estate licensing law is

    A. a fraud
    B. a misrepresentation
    C. a misdemeanor
    D. prosecuted by the district attorney

8. A real estate contract must be

   A. in writing
   B. recorded
   C. for more than 3 years
   D. oral

9. A metes and bounds description is a

   A. description by street number
   B. description indicating measurements and boundaries
   C. description by monument
   D. block, lot, and section description

10. A written power of attorney may be used to authorize another person to sign a contract, deed, or mortgage on his behalf. In such a case,

    A. the one authorized is required to have a real estate license if he receives a fee
    B. no license is required
    C. the one authorized must be a lawyer
    D. brokers are disqualified from acting under a power of attorney

11. Absolute ownership of real property is called

    A. estate for life
    B. estate by the entirety
    C. remainder estate
    D. fee simple

12. The purpose of the real estate licensing law is to

    A. govern the real estate board
    B. regulate the commissions which brokers charge
    C. protect brokers
    D. protect the public from dishonest and incompetent brokers

13. When a broker puts a client's money into his own account,

    A. it is perfectly proper
    B. it is called commingling
    C. it is proper only if he returns the money to the client upon request
    D. he is guilty of violating the real estate licensing law

14. The usual type of deed which a buyer receives in a conveyance is a _____ deed.

    A. referee's
    B. bargain and sale
    C. quit claim
    D. full covenant and warranty

15. Transfer of all of the tenant's rights in a lease is called a(n)

    A. sublease
    B. assignment
    C. option
    D. power of attorney

16. Money or a deed held in escrow at a title closing is for the benefit of

    A. buyer only
    B. seller only

C. buyer and the seller
D. the seller or buyer if they are under 21 years of age

17. A tenant agrees to pay the rent plus all the expenses. This is known as a _____ lease.

    A. net B. gross C. tenant's D. graduated

18. A real estate broker arranges the sale of a parcel of real property for the price asked by the seller. It is discovered that he was in a position to sell the property to another purchaser at a higher price, which he deliberately failed to do.
    Under the above conditions, the broker would be entitled to

    A. the full commission
    B. one-half of the commission
    C. no commission
    D. the full commission less the difference in the selling price and the higher price offered

19. A listing of real property with a number of brokers is called a(n) _____ listing.

    A. open B. multiple C. exclusive D. implied

20. A limitation placed upon the use of property is called a

    A. lis pendens   B. violation
    C. restriction   D. lien

21. A report on the condition of ownership is a(n)

    A. abstract of title
    B. survey report
    C. county clerk's authentication
    D. title policy

22. The overhang or projection of a foundation wall, a porch, or a balcony beyond the established line of a parcel of land is known as a(n)

    A. violation   B. easement
    C. encroachment   D. restriction

23. A contract based on an illegal consideration is

    A. valid   B. void
    C. legal   D. enforceable

24. West, a prospective buyer, writes a letter on October 15 to Wilder, a property owner, and prospective seller offering to buy Wilder's property for $40,000.00. Wilder replies promptly by letter stating, *I accept your offer contained in your letter of 10/15.*
    Which of the following MOST accurately describes the situation? There is

    A. an offer but no acceptance
    B. a valid contract between the parties
    C. an acceptance but no offer
    D. no contract between the parties

25. One of the ESSENTIAL elements of a valid contract of sale of real estate is

   A. money-back guarantee
   B. clear title
   C. consideration
   D. market value

KEY (CORRECT ANSWERS)

1. C
2. B
3. A
4. D
5. C

6. B
7. C
8. A
9. B
10. B

11. D
12. D
13. B
14. B
15. B

16. C
17. A
18. C
19. A
20. C

21. A
22. C
23. B
24. D
25. B

TEST 2

DIRECTIONS: Each question or incomplete statement is followed by several suggested answers or completions. Select the one that BEST answers the question or completes the statement. *PRINT THE LETTER OF THE CORRECT ANSWER IN THE SPACE AT THE RIGHT.*

1. A real estate broker's license was suspended but he continued to do business. He negotiated the sale of a parcel of real property and, upon completion of his services, made a claim for the commission earned.
   Under these circumstances, the commission is payable to

   A. the courts B. the broker
   C. the purchaser D. no one

2. Every person licensed as a real estate broker shall

   A. have and maintain a post office box
   B. have and maintain a definite place of business
   C. be actively engaged in the real estate business
   D. file a trade name certificate

3. A licensed salesman severs his connections with his employing broker. The salesman's license, which is in the custody of the broker, should be

   A. returned to the real estate licensing board
   B. used for a new employee
   C. kept on file by the broker
   D. destroyed by the broker

4. The deed used in any involuntary transfer of real property is a(n) _____ deed.

   A. bargain and sale B. executor's
   C. referee's D. quit claim

5. One who bequeaths real property by will is called a(n)

   A. grantee   B. devisee   C. assignee   D. devisor

6. By a covenant against the grantor's acts, the seller represents that

   A. he will hold the consideration as a trust fund for any improvement made thereon
   B. the property is free of liens
   C. he has done nothing to render the title unmarketable
   D. no dower attaches to the property

7. Property of a person who dies intestate, leaving no heirs, passes to the state by

   A. adverse possession B. condemnation
   C. eminent domain D. escheat

8. The covenant which makes it mandatory that the seller execute any additional instruments necessary to perfect the title at any future date is called the

   A. covenant of seizin
   B. covenant of further assurance

101

C. covenant of quiet enjoyment
D. encumbrance covenant

9. The right to convey ownership to another is the right of

   A. dispossession
   B. consideration
   C. alienation
   D. equity

10. An action to take private property for public use with compensation to the owner is called a(n)

    A. lis pendens
    B. specific performance
    C. condemnation proceeding
    D. escheat

11. A widow is willed the use of the family house for the rest of her natural life, with the provision that upon her death it shall pass to her son. The son is called the

    A. life tenant
    B. holder in due course
    C. remainderman
    D. tenant in common

12. A real estate broker is the holder of a sixty-day exclusive agency for the sale of a parcel of real property.
    At the end of thirty days, the owner of the property dies. The broker, with only one-half of his exclusive agency expired, should

    A. claim one-half of the commission from the estate
    B. continue his efforts to sell for the balance of his agreement
    C. refer to the owner's death in his advertising
    D. discontinue his efforts to sell

13. If the contract of sale does not state a time for closing, then it is intended that the closing of title be

    A. postponed indefinitely
    B. within 60 days
    C. within a reasonable time
    D. within one month

14. Any right to or interest in real property that diminishes its value is called an

    A. estoppel
    B. amortization agreement
    C. abstract
    D. encumbrance

15. Title to chattels are usually conveyed by a

    A. quit claim deed
    B. bill of sale
    C. writ of ownership
    D. certificate of title

16. The right or privilege granted to an individual to go from his lands on, over, and through the land of another is called a(n)

    A. easement
    B. encroachment
    C. lis pendens
    D. escrow

17. A signed receipt reading as follows was given to a prospective purchaser of five lots in a subdivision: *Received from John Jones the sum of $50,000 on account of the purchase of five lots in Block X, balance $450,000; deed to be delivered on July 1, 2008.*
John Jones has the right to refuse to complete his purchase because

    A. the receipt is not dated
    B. the type of deed is not mentioned
    C. there is no proper description
    D. the point that time is of the essence was not mentioned

18. In the purchase of real property, upon which there is already an existing mortgage, it is generally ADVISABLE for the purchaser to _____ the mortgage.

    A. foreclose on   B. assume
    C. assign   D. buy subject to

19. The evidence of a personal debt which is secured by a lien on real estate is called

    A. mortgage   B. bond
    C. trust deed   D. deficiency

20. The operation of paying off a mortgage by periodic installments is called _____ the mortgage.

    A. prepaying   B. subordinating
    C. amortizing   D. depreciating

21. The clause in a blanket mortgage that allows the mortgagor to acquire unencumbered title to part of the property upon part payment of the mortgage is the _____ clause.

    A. acceleration   B. prepayment
    C. partial release   D. amortization

22. Mortgages that permit flexible borrowing to permit future additions or alterations are known as _____ mortgages.

    A. purchase money   B. open-end
    C. subordination   D. open

23. When a tenancy is terminable at the volition of either party, the tenancy is known as a

    A. tenancy at will   B. tenancy at sufferance
    C. monthly tenancy   D. statutory tenancy

24. Seizure of personal property by court order, usually done to have it available in the event a judgment is obtained in a pending suit, is called a(n)

    A. foreclosure   B. lien
    C. reversion   D. attachment

25. The law which requires that a contract for the sale of real property be in writing is called

    A. the Statute of Limitations
    B. the Real Property Law
    C. the Statute of Frauds
    D. the Law of Eminent Domain

KEY (CORRECT ANSWERS)

1. D
2. B
3. A
4. C
5. D

6. B
7. D
8. B
9. C
10. C

11. C
12. D
13. C
14. D
15. B

16. A
17. C
18. D
19. A
20. C

21. C
22. B
23. A
24. D
25. C

EXAMINATION SECTION
TEST 1

DIRECTIONS: Each question or incomplete statement is followed by several suggested answers or completions. Select the one that BEST answers the question or completes the statement. *PRINT THE LETTER OF THE CORRECT ANSWER IN THE SPACE AT THE RIGHT.*

1. A lease for more than one year must be

    A. recorded
    B. acknowledged
    C. in writing
    D. delivered

    1.____

2. Money given on a binder is called

    A. an option
    B. earnest money
    C. an escrow
    D. a listing

    2.____

3. The broker refuses commission. The salesman may sue

    A. the broker
    B. the seller
    C. the broker and the seller
    D. no one

    3.____

4. Who does NOT need a real estate license?

    A. A lawyer who hires salesmen
    B. One who sells listings
    C. An auctioneer of real estate
    D. A referee in a foreclosure

    4.____

5. In the foreclosure of a tax lien, the buyer receives a(n)

    A. bargain and sale deed
    B. full covenant and warranty deed
    C. referee's deed
    D. administrator's deed

    5.____

6. A salesman discontinues his employment with a broker. He must

    A. obtain his broker's consent
    B. notify the real estate licensing board
    C. return his license
    D. do nothing

    6.____

7. A violation of the real estate licensing law is

    A. a fraud
    B. a misrepresentation
    C. a misdemeanor
    D. prosecuted by the district attorney

    7.____

8. A real estate contract must be

   A. in writing
   B. recorded
   C. for more than 3 years
   D. oral

9. A metes and bounds description is a

   A. description by street number
   B. description indicating measurements and boundaries
   C. description by monument
   D. block, lot, and section description

10. A written power of attorney may be used to authorize another person to sign a contract, deed, or mortgage on his behalf. In such a case,

    A. the one authorized is required to have a real estate license if he receives a fee
    B. no license is required
    C. the one authorized must be a lawyer
    D. brokers are disqualified from acting under a power of attorney

11. Absolute ownership of real property is called

    A. estate for life
    B. estate by the entirety
    C. remainder estate
    D. fee simple

12. The purpose of the real estate licensing law is to

    A. govern the real estate board
    B. regulate the commissions which brokers charge
    C. protect brokers
    D. protect the public from dishonest and incompetent brokers

13. When a broker puts a client's money into his own account,

    A. it is perfectly proper
    B. it is called commingling
    C. it is proper only if he returns the money to the client upon request
    D. he is guilty of violating the real estate licensing law

14. The usual type of deed which a buyer receives in a conveyance is a _____ deed.

    A. referee's
    B. bargain and sale
    C. quit claim
    D. full covenant and warranty

15. Transfer of all of the tenant's rights in a lease is called a(n)

    A. sublease
    B. assignment
    C. option
    D. power of attorney

16. Money or a deed held in escrow at a title closing is for the benefit of

    A. buyer only
    B. seller only

C. buyer and the seller
D. the seller or buyer if they are under 21 years of age

17. A tenant agrees to pay the rent plus all the expenses. This is known as a _____ lease.

    A. net   B. gross   C. tenant's   D. graduated

18. A real estate broker arranges the sale of a parcel of real property for the price asked by the seller. It is discovered that he was in a position to sell the property to another purchaser at a higher price, which he deliberately failed to do.
    Under the above conditions, the broker would be entitled to

    A. the full commission
    B. one-half of the commission
    C. no commission
    D. the full commission less the difference in the selling price and the higher price offered

19. A listing of real property with a number of brokers is called a(n) _____ listing.

    A. open   B. multiple   C. exclusive   D. implied

20. A limitation placed upon the use of property is called a

    A. lis pendens   B. violation
    C. restriction   D. lien

21. A report on the condition of ownership is a(n)

    A. abstract of title
    B. survey report
    C. county clerk's authentication
    D. title policy

22. The overhang or projection of a foundation wall, a porch, or a balcony beyond the established line of a parcel of land is known as a(n)

    A. violation   B. easement
    C. encroachment   D. restriction

23. A contract based on an illegal consideration is

    A. valid   B. void
    C. legal   D. enforceable

24. West, a prospective buyer, writes a letter on October 15 to Wilder, a property owner, and prospective seller offering to buy Wilder's property for $40,000.00. Wilder replies promptly by letter stating, *I accept your offer contained in your letter of 10/15.* Which of the following MOST accurately describes the situation? There is

    A. an offer but no acceptance
    B. a valid contract between the parties
    C. an acceptance but no offer
    D. no contract between the parties

25. One of the ESSENTIAL elements of a valid contract of sale of real estate is

    A. money-back guarantee   B. clear title
    C. consideration   D. market value

KEY (CORRECT ANSWERS)

1. C
2. B
3. A
4. D
5. C
6. B
7. C
8. A
9. B
10. B
11. D
12. D
13. B
14. B
15. B
16. C
17. A
18. C
19. A
20. C
21. A
22. C
23. B
24. D
25. B

TEST 2

DIRECTIONS: Each question or incomplete statement is followed by several suggested answers or completions. Select the one that BEST answers the question or completes the statement. *PRINT THE LETTER OF THE CORRECT ANSWER IN THE SPACE AT THE RIGHT.*

1. A real estate broker's license was suspended but he continued to do business. He negotiated the sale of a parcel of real property and, upon completion of his services, made a claim for the commission earned.
   Under these circumstances, the commission is payable to

   A. the courts B. the broker
   C. the purchaser D. no one

2. Every person licensed as a real estate broker shall

   A. have and maintain a post office box
   B. have and maintain a definite place of business
   C. be actively engaged in the real estate business
   D. file a trade name certificate

3. A licensed salesman severs his connections with his employing broker. The salesman's license, which is in the custody of the broker, should be

   A. returned to the real estate licensing board
   B. used for a new employee
   C. kept on file by the broker
   D. destroyed by the broker

4. The deed used in any involuntary transfer of real property is a(n) _____ deed.

   A. bargain and sale B. executor's
   C. referee's D. quit claim

5. One who bequeaths real property by will is called a(n)

   A. grantee B. devisee C. assignee D. devisor

6. By a covenant against the grantor's acts, the seller represents that

   A. he will hold the consideration as a trust fund for any improvement made thereon
   B. the property is free of liens
   C. he has done nothing to render the title unmarketable
   D. no dower attaches to the property

7. Property of a person who dies intestate, leaving no heirs, passes to the state by

   A. adverse possession B. condemnation
   C. eminent domain D. escheat

8. The covenant which makes it mandatory that the seller execute any additional instruments necessary to perfect the title at any future date is called the

   A. covenant of seizin
   B. covenant of further assurance

109

C. covenant of quiet enjoyment
D. encumbrance covenant

9. The right to convey ownership to another is the right of

   A. dispossession
   B. consideration
   C. alienation
   D. equity

10. An action to take private property for public use with compensation to the owner is called a(n)

    A. lis pendens
    B. specific performance
    C. condemnation proceeding
    D. escheat

11. A widow is willed the use of the family house for the rest of her natural life, with the provision that upon her death it shall pass to her son. The son is called the

    A. life tenant
    B. holder in due course
    C. remainderman
    D. tenant in common

12. A real estate broker is the holder of a sixty-day exclusive agency for the sale of a parcel of real property.
    At the end of thirty days, the owner of the property dies. The broker, with only one-half of his exclusive agency expired, should

    A. claim one-half of the commission from the estate
    B. continue his efforts to sell for the balance of his agreement
    C. refer to the owner's death in his advertising
    D. discontinue his efforts to sell

13. If the contract of sale does not state a time for closing, then it is intended that the closing of title be

    A. postponed indefinitely
    B. within 60 days
    C. within a reasonable time
    D. within one month

14. Any right to or interest in real property that diminishes its value is called an

    A. estoppel
    B. amortization agreement
    C. abstract
    D. encumbrance

15. Title to chattels are usually conveyed by a

    A. quit claim deed
    B. bill of sale
    C. writ of ownership
    D. certificate of title

16. The right or privilege granted to an individual to go from his lands on, over, and through the land of another is called a(n)

    A. easement
    B. encroachment
    C. lis pendens
    D. escrow

17. A signed receipt reading as follows was given to a prospective purchaser of five lots in a subdivision: *Received from John Jones the sum of $50,000 on account of the purchase of five lots in Block X, balance $450,000; deed to be delivered on July 1, 2008.* John Jones has the right to refuse to complete his purchase because

    A. the receipt is not dated
    B. the type of deed is not mentioned
    C. there is no proper description
    D. the point that time is of the essence was not mentioned

17.____

18. In the purchase of real property, upon which there is already an existing mortgage, it is generally ADVISABLE for the purchaser to _____ the mortgage.

    A. foreclose on B. assume
    C. assign   D. buy subject to

18.____

19. The evidence of a personal debt which is secured by a lien on real estate is called

    A. mortgage   B. bond
    C. trust deed D. deficiency

19.____

20. The operation of paying off a mortgage by periodic installments is called _____ the mortgage.

    A. prepaying   B. subordinating
    C. amortizing D. depreciating

20.____

21. The clause in a blanket mortgage that allows the mortgagor to acquire unencumbered title to part of the property upon part payment of the mortgage is the _____ clause.

    A. acceleration   B. prepayment
    C. partial release D. amortization

21.____

22. Mortgages that permit flexible borrowing to permit future additions or alterations are known as _____ mortgages.

    A. purchase money B. open-end
    C. subordination   D. open

22.____

23. When a tenancy is terminable at the volition of either party, the tenancy is known as a

    A. tenancy at will B. tenancy at sufferance
    C. monthly tenancy D. statutory tenancy

23.____

24. Seizure of personal property by court order, usually done to have it available in the event a judgment is obtained in a pending suit, is called a(n)

    A. foreclosure B. lien
    C. reversion   D. attachment

24.____

25. The law which requires that a contract for the sale of real property be in writing is called

    A. the Statute of Limitations
    B. the Real Property Law
    C. the Statute of Frauds
    D. the Law of Eminent Domain

25.____

KEY (CORRECT ANSWERS)

1. D
2. B
3. A
4. C
5. D

6. B
7. D
8. B
9. C
10. C

11. C
12. D
13. C
14. D
15. B

16. A
17. C
18. D
19. A
20. C

21. C
22. B
23. A
24. D
25. C

EXAMINATION SECTION
TEST 1

DIRECTIONS: Each question or incomplete statement is followed by several suggested answers or completions. Select the one that BEST answers the question or completes the statement. *PRINT THE LETTER OF THE CORRECT ANSWER IN THE SPACE AT THE RIGHT.*

1. When using the cost depreciation approach, value equals

    A. the reconciled value of comparables
    B. income divided by the capitalization rate
    C. vacant land value plus depreciated building value
    D. gross income times the standard multiplier

    1.____

2. Which of the following is CORRECT concerning appraisers?

    A. An appraiser's license is necessary
    B. They are compensated on a fee basis according to the difficulty of their assignment
    C. They search for market price
    D. All of the above

    2.____

3. When the question of title arises, the broker should

    A. be sure to base any statement he makes upon his opinion only
    B. do nothing since brokers have no duty to the prospect because there is no fiduciary relationship
    C. advise the prospect to procure an abstract to be examined by a competent attorney or obtain title insurance
    D. tell the prospect to seek the seller's opinion

    3.____

4. A broker may have a branch office

    A. near his main office
    B. anywhere in the country
    C. in his home
    D. all of the above

    4.____

5. A broker has fiduciary duties because he

    A. is licensed
    B. adheres to a code of ethics
    C. is responsible to his principal
    D. is bound by contract

    5.____

6. A broker has a listing for $10,000.00. He obtains an offer of $12,000.00. The broker buys the property for $10,000.00 and resells it for $12,000.00.
   This is a(n)

    A. conspiracy
    B. overage
    C. illegal commission
    D. lawful practice

    6.____

7. A salesperson can have an escrow account

    A. in the normal course of business
    B. only with the approval of his employer

    7.____

C. only with the approval of his employer and the licensing commission
D. under no circumstances

8. Which of the following statements BEST describes the relationship between the broker and his prospect?

    A. They are dealing at arm's length.
    B. The broker must report any facts or rumors concerning the property.
    C. They are governed by the rule *caveat emptor.*
    D. The prospect can rely upon material statements.

9. A salesperson selling his own property

    A. must have the broker place the ad and need not state that he is a registered salesperson
    B. can advertise in his own name and need not state that he is a registered salesperson
    C. can avoid the rule about advertising in the broker's name and advertise as for sale by owner, indicating that he is a registered salesperson and giving his employer's telephone number
    D. must have the broker place the ad and give the broker's and salesperson's names

10. If a broker wishes to obtain a true option, he must

    A. pay a definite, valuable consideration
    B. divest himself of his identity as a broker
    C. pay a definite valuable consideration and divest himself of his identity as a broker
    D. do no more than any other purchaser

11. Which of the following is(are) CORRECT?
    I. A contract for sale of a homestead requires two witnesses.
    II. An individual must file annually for homestead exemption.
    The CORRECT answer is:

    A. I *only*
    B. II *only*
    C. Both I and II
    D. Neither I nor II

12. Eminent domain is thought of in connection with

    A. courts
    B. the government
    C. private enterprise
    D. death intestate with no heirs

13. An encumbrance affects

    A. existing mortgages
    B. title
    C. possession
    D. zoning

14. The secret sale of more than one-half of a business's assets is prevented by the

    A. Fictitious Names Act
    B. State Real Estate License Law
    C. Division of State Land Sales
    D. Bulk Sales Act

15. Which of the following are proof of merchantable title?   15.____

    A. Abstract and survey
    B. Abstract and title insurance
    C. Title insurance and survey
    D. None of the above

16. Which of the following is(are) CORRECT?   16.____
    A(n)
        I. abstract is an assurance of clear title
        II. title search required for closing always takes place on the day of closing; therefore, the buyer is protected when he receives the deed
    The CORRECT answer is:

    A. I *only*   B. II *only*
    C. Both I and II   D. Neither I nor II

17. The mortgage insurance premium for the insurance on FHA 203(b) loans is   17.____

    A. one-half of 1 percent of the remaining principal balance payable monthly
    B. paid with the annual casualty insurance premium
    C. one-half of 1 percent of the monthly payment
    D. paid with the discount at the closing

18. The PRIMARY concern of any real estate investment should be   18.____

    A. tax shelter aspects   B. depreciation deductions
    C. economic soundness   D. location

19. Which of the following are INCORRECT concerning mortgages?   19.____

    A. Signed by the mortgagee
    B. Signed by two witnesses
    C. Signed by the mortgagor
    D. Both A and B

20. Broker Brown receives three offers on a parcel of property he has listed. Two of the offers were oral.   20.____
    In order to PROPERLY serve his employer, he must submit

    A. the offers in the order he received them
    B. only the written offer
    C. only those offers accompanied by a binder deposit
    D. all of the offers regardless of form, binder deposit, price, or order in which they were received

KEY (CORRECT ANSWERS)

1.	C	11.	D
2.	B	12.	B
3.	C	13.	B
4.	D	14.	D
5.	A	15.	D
6.	B	16.	D
7.	D	17.	D
8.	D	18.	C
9.	B	19.	D
10.	C	20.	D

TEST 2

DIRECTIONS: Each question or incomplete statement is followed by several suggested answers or completions. Select the one that BEST answers the question or completes the statement. *PRINT THE LETTER OF THE CORRECT ANSWER IN THE SPACE AT THE RIGHT.*

1. A contract with a promise of performance on one side is called a(n) _____ contract.   1.____

   A. implied
   B. bilateral
   C. executed
   D. unilateral

2. The passage or amendment of rules by the licensing commission is an exercise of which power?   2.____

   A. Executive
   B. Quasi-legislative
   C. Ministerial
   D. Quasi-judicial

3. Which of the following is probably NOT real estate?   3.____
   A

   A. tree
   B. refrigerator
   C. lease
   D. fence

4. Prior to acceptance of the offer, the earnest money deposit is under control of the   4.____

   A. broker
   B. seller
   C. broker and buyer-depositor
   D. buyer-depositor

5. A purchaser signs an offer stating that he wishes to offer $65,000 for a home listed for $67,000. His offer is accepted and signed by the offeree. Prior to being notified of the acceptance, the purchaser enters into an agreement to purchase another property. Which of the following applies?   5.____

   A. If the purchaser revokes the $65,000 offer prior to being notified of the acceptance of the offer, no breach of contract has occurred.
   B. The purchaser has breached the contract because offers must remain in effect for a reasonable length of time.
   C. The purchaser will be found guilty of fraud because this is a direct violation of the Statute of Frauds.
   D. Both B and C are correct.

6. If a seller of property did not receive all money due him and did not receive security for that unpaid money, he is eligible for a   6.____

   A. lis pendens
   B. second mortgage
   C. mechanic's lien
   D. vendor's lien

7. Which of the following business organizations can register as a broker?   7.____

   A. Corporation not for profit
   B. Corporation for profit
   C. Corporation sole
   D. Cooperative association

8. Broker A pays $50 for a 90-day option to owner Owen. The agreed-upon price is $100,000. On the 60th day, broker A finds a purchaser for the property at a sales price of $130,000. Broker A exercises his option and sells the property for $130,000. Which of the following applies?

   A. Broker A is entitled to a $30,000 profit
   B. Broker A has violated his fiduciary duties and is liable
   C. Broker A will have to share his profit
   D. None of the above

9. The right granted by a property owner to another to enter upon that owner's property is known as an

   A. encumbrance
   B. easement
   C. encroachment
   D. escheat

10. Real estate salesmen may be employed by

    A. owners *only*
    B. brokers *only*
    C. broker or owner-employer
    D. none of the above

11. A deed warranting title only against claims of the grantor, his heirs, assigns, executors, or administrators, and others claiming by or through him is called a _____ deed.

    A. general warranty
    B. bargain and sale
    C. quit-claim
    D. special warranty

12. Brokers A and B are partners in developing a parcel of land. C, a licensed salesperson, later purchases a share of the partnership. All proceeds from the sale of the developed land are divided according to ownership shares. Which of the following is CORRECT?

    A. C must be a broker to become a true partner.
    B. The salesperson must be inactive.
    C. No registration with the licensing commission is necessary.
    D. This partnership must register with the licensing commission.

13. In order to reduce the risk inherent in originating high loan-to-value ratio loans, lenders require

    A. increased interest rates
    B. mortgage insurance
    C. discount
    D. all of the above

14. Prior to the marriage, real estate owned by a husband or wife is presumed to be

    A. in a joint estate
    B. in a tenancy in common
    C. in an estate by the entireties
    D. separate property

15. The mortgagor's right to bring himself out of default by paying money owed to the lender is called

    A. the assumption of mortgage
    B. the amortization of mortgage
    C. the equity of redemption
    D. strict foreclosure

16. A mentally incompetent person may act as a grantor and deliver title to his own property by signing a _____ deed. 16.____

    A. guardian's
    B. committee's
    C. quit-claim
    D. none of the above

17. A member of the licensing commission may serve no more than _____ years. 17.____

    A. four
    B. eight
    C. ten
    D. none of the above

18. A written offer to purchase is submitted to a seller and he, in turn, changes the terms or conditions, initials the changes, signs the instrument, and sends it back to the offeror. In the law of contracts, this is a(n) 18.____

    A. offer
    B. binding offer
    C. irrevocable offer
    D. counteroffer

19. How many acres are contained in the N 1/2 of the SW 1/4 of the SE 1/4 of the NE 1/4 of Section 9? 19.____
    _____ acres.

    A. 10
    B. 5
    C. 2 1/2
    D. 1 1/4

20. Negative taxable income is known as 20.____

    A. capital gain
    B. cash flow
    C. debt service
    D. tax shelter

KEY (CORRECT ANSWERS)

1.	D	11.	D
2.	B	12.	C
3.	B	13.	B
4.	D	14.	D
5.	A	15.	C
6.	D	16.	D
7.	B	17.	D
8.	B	18.	D
9.	B	19.	B
10.	C	20.	D

TEST 3

DIRECTIONS: Each question or incomplete statement is followed by several suggested answers or completions. Select the one that BEST answers the question or completes the statement. *PRINT THE LETTER OF THE CORRECT ANSWER IN THE SPACE AT THE RIGHT.*

1. During periods of disintermediation in the primary mortgage market, the mortgage money supply

    A. is unaffected
    B. decreases
    C. increases
    D. either increases or decreases, according to demand

2. Under the income approach to appraisal, value equals

    A. vacant land value plus depreciated building value
    B. rate times income
    C. rate divided by income
    D. income divided by rate

3. A and B form a business in which A is totally liable for any debts which are incurred, but B is only liable to the extent of his investment.
   This is PROBABLY a

    A. corporation   B. general partnership
    C. joint venture   D. limited partnership

4. Brokers are permitted to draw leases

    A. in the normal course of their business
    B. if power of attorney is granted to the owner
    C. never
    D. only if the brokers divest

5. The license of a broker is revoked.
   Licenses of salespeople employed by that broker are

    A. revoked   B. suspended
    C. reprimanded   D. canceled

6. Which of the following may involve the securities laws as well as the real estate laws?

    A. Condominiums
    B. Sales of real estate by transfer of stock of a corporation
    C. Group investment
    D. All of the above

7. Finders' fees paid to unlicensed individuals

    A. are illegal
    B. are simply poor business practices
    C. should be made to stimulate referrals
    D. are not illegal

8. Qualifying refers to

   A. lender analyzing borrower and property
   B. salesperson determining a prospect's needs and capabilities
   C. broker checking up on past clients
   D. both A and B

Questions 9-12.

DIRECTIONS: Questions 9 through 12 are to be answered on the basis of the following passage.

John is a salesperson working for Ann, the broker. John obtains a written offer and a deposit on a property listed with the office. He deposits the money in his own account, indicating that it is to be held in escrow for the buyer. The seller accepts the offer, and John writes a check to his broker for the deposit. She deposits the check in her business account. The buyer defaults, and Ann divides the escrow deposit with John.

9. What should John have done with the deposit money?

   A. Exactly what he did since the problem is the action taken by Ann, the broker
   B. Left it in his own escrow account
   C. Immediately turned it over to his broker
   D. Held it until the offer was accepted, then turned it over to his broker

10. What should Ann have done when she received the deposit?

    A. Exactly what she did since the buyer and seller agreed to it
    B. Immediately deposited it in her escrow account
    C. Returned the money to the buyer
    D. Left the money in John's escrow account

11. Which of the following is(are) CORRECT?
    I. John is guilty of conversion.
    II. Ann is guilty of conversion.

    The CORRECT answer is:

    A. I *only*   B. II *only*
    C. Both I and II   D. Neither I nor II

12. Assuming that the money had been handled properly up until the time of default by the buyer, what should Ann do upon the buyer's default?

    A. Return the deposit
    B. Exactly what she did
    C. Divide the money equally with John and the seller
    D. Divide the money with the seller according to their agreement and divide her share with John according to their agreement

13. A first-degree misdemeanor will be imposed by courts as a result of

    A. violations of advance fee accounting requirements or false advertising
    B. payment made from the Recovery Fund
    C. any violation of law
    D. B and C are correct

14. Owner A lists 1000 acres with broker B, and specifies the price and terms he will accept. B discovers that by selling on the price and terms stated, A will be liable for a large amount of income tax.
    B should

    A. change the listing for the protection of the principal
    B. tell A nothing because he has nothing to do with income tax
    C. follow the instructions of the principal
    D. advise A of this and tell him to seek the advice of an income tax expert

15. Which of the following shares of real property will a widow with no children receive at her husband's death in the absence of a will?

    A. One-third   B. All   C. One-half   D. None

16. An estate held by two or more parties in which each has equal or proportionate rights as to possession, enjoyment, and the time and duration, having the same or different origin, is being held as a(n)

    A. estate for years
    B. joint estate
    C. estate by the entireties
    D. tenancy in common

17. A seller agrees to deliver to a buyer a perfect record title. Examination of the abstract by a competent attorney reveals breaks in the chain of title.
    The seller would then do which of the following?

    A. Buy title insurance for the buyer
    B. File a suit to quiet title
    C. Get an affidavit from the Clerk of the Circuit Court attesting to his knowledge and belief that the seller's title is good
    D. Transfer title by quit-claim deed

18. A broker-salesperson employed by more than one owner should

    A. apply for a multiple license
    B. apply for a group license
    C. broker-salesperson may not be employed by an owner
    D. none of the above

19. If all rights under a lease are subrogated, the result is

    A. a sublease   B. an assignment
    C. a violation of law   D. either A or B

20. A broker may collect a commission when he has negotiated a sale of property with the knowledge and consent of the owner even though no previous express listing was given the broker on the basis that he had a(n)

   A. open listing
   B. true option
   C. implied listing
   D. option which should be treated as a listing

20._____

KEY (CORRECT ANSWERS)

1.	B	11.	C
2.	D	12.	D
3.	D	13.	A
4.	C	14.	D
5.	D	15.	B
6.	D	16.	D
7.	A	17.	B
8.	D	18.	D
9.	C	19.	B
10.	B	20.	C

TEST 4

DIRECTIONS: Each question or incomplete statement is followed by several suggested answers or completions. Select the one that BEST answers the question or completes the statement. *PRINT THE LETTER OF THE CORRECT ANSWER IN THE SPACE AT THE RIGHT.*

1. If a grantor in a deed is insolvent, a quit-claim deed is as desirable as a _____ deed. 1.___

    A. bargain and sale
    B. special warranty
    C. general warranty
    D. all of the above

2. What is the government survey method description of the property shown at the right? 2.___

    A. NE 1/4 of the NE 1/4 of the SW 1/4 of Section 8
    B. NW 1/4 of the NW 1/4 of the SW 1/4 of Section 8
    C. N 1/2 of the NE 1/4 of the SE 1/4 of Section 8
    D. SW 1/4 of the NE 1/4 of the NE 1/4 of Section 8

3. A violation of law may result in 3.___

    A. imprisonment
    B. injunction
    C. suspension
    D. all of the above

4. The mortgage lien remains in effect until 4.___

    A. the note is paid in full
    B. defeasance clause is satisfied
    C. a satisfaction is signed and recorded
    D. all of the above

5. An exclusive listing 5.___

    A. guarantees the listing broker a commission if the property is sold through another broker
    B. must be in writing
    C. is given to only one broker
    D. all of the above

6. A broker sells a prospective tenant a rental list for $100. The prospective tenant inspected all the properties and found them to be occupied. The tenant then demanded a full refund; what action should the broker take? 6.___

    A. Refund $100
    B. Refund $25
    C. Refund $75
    D. No refund should be made

7. A license is 7.___

    A. prima facie evidence of licensure
    B. issued for a period not to exceed two years
    C. proof of residency
    D. both A and B

8. B wants a motel site, and salesperson A showed him a good location which was zoned for a motel. A then went on vacation. Upon A's return, B purchased the site with A's assistance. A did not know that while he was on vacation the zoning had been changed, and B was subsequently denied a building permit for his motel.
   Which applies?

   A. A is guilty of nothing as there was no intent.
   B. A is guilty of negligence and may be disciplined.
   C. A and his broker are both guilty of fraud and may be disciplined.
   D. A is guilty of culpable negligence and subject to discipline.

9. When a broker represents two parties in a transaction,

   A. he must have the consent of both parties in order to collect a dual commission
   B. he must disclose his agency to both parties
   C. he may not represent two parties with adverse interests in a transaction
   D. both A and B are correct

10. When the license period is about to expire, the licensee should apply for a renewal. The effective date for that renewal will be the date

    A. the licensee makes the proper application to the department
    B. the department receives the application in proper form with proper fee attached
    C. following the expiration date of the original license
    D. the licensee receives the license

11. When a dispute arises concerning the disposition of escrowed funds and the broker is the escrow agent, the broker's FIRST action should be to

    A. ask the licensing commission for an Escrow Disbursement Order
    B. give the deposit to the seller
    C. collect his portion of the deposit as damages
    D. notify the licensing commission

12. Which of the following is(are) CORRECT?
    I. All officers and directors of real estate corporations must be brokers
    II. All partners in a real estate partnership must be brokers
    The CORRECT answer is:

    A. I only
    B. II only
    C. Both I and II
    D. Neither I nor II

13. Paul, a service station owner, has been appointed by a court to appraise another service station. Paul has no real estate license.
    Which of the following applies?

    A. He may apply to the licensing commission for a special exception.
    B. He may appraise the property only if he is knowledgeable as to its value.
    C. He must appraise the property while under the supervision of a licensed real estate broker.
    D. He may be compensated for appraising the property.

14. Using borrowed money to finance the purchase of real estate is known as

   A. larceny
   B. conversion
   C. leverage
   D. commingling

15. A licensee who appeals a decision by the real estate commission regarding a disciplinary decision may have his license privileges restored by

   A. injunction
   B. warrant
   C. the hearing officer
   D. writ of mandamus

16. Concerning the collection of advance fees, the broker should place

   A. 75 percent in escrow to be used for the benefit of the principal
   B. 100 percent in escrow
   C. 25 percent in escrow to be used for the benefit of the principal
   D. 100 percent in escrow to be used for the benefit of the principal

17. In order for a salesperson to become a successful broker applicant, he must

   A. work for one active broker for one year as an active salesperson
   B. complete the required educational course for broker
   C. work for one active broker or an owner-employer for one year as an active salesperson
   D. both A and B are correct

18. Which of the following is(are) CORRECT?
   I. If the first mortgage is paid off and satisfied, the second mortgage becomes the first.
   II. Both husband and wife must execute a satisfaction of mortgage when the mortgage is held in the husband's name only.

   The CORRECT answer is:

   A. I *only*
   B. II *only*
   C. Both I and II
   D. Neither I nor II

19. Broker Alice and broker Bob formed a partnership to provide real estate services for others. Broker Alice converts funds and has her license suspended.
   Which applies?

   A. Listings held by the partnership have been terminated
   B. The partnership license has been canceled
   C. Salespeople working for the partnership should obtain a reissue of their license under a new employer if they desire to continue operating
   D. All of the above

20. A real estate salesperson wishes to incorporate to buy, develop, and sell real estate. Which of the following BEST applies?

   A. He must obtain a broker's license.
   B. He must register the corporation with the real estate commission.
   C. No license is necessary.
   D. Both A and B are correct.

KEY (CORRECT ANSWERS)

1.	D	11.	D
2.	A	12.	D
3.	D	13.	D
4.	C	14.	C
5.	C	15.	D
6.	A	16.	A
7.	D	17.	B
8.	D	18.	A
9.	C	19.	D
10.	C	20.	C

EXAMINATION SECTION
TEST 1

DIRECTIONS: In continuous discourse, briefly and concisely answer the following questions.

1. Who are real estate brokers within the meaning of the Act?
2. What is meant by the word "compensation" as used in the definition of real estate broker?
3. Does the term "Valuable consideration" as used in the definition of a real estate broker, mean only a money consideration?
4. Does the term "real estate" as used in the Act refer only to the land itself, without improvements?
5. Does one engaged in the business of real property management come within the Act?
6. What is meant by the term "associate real estate broker"?
7. What is meant by the term "real estate salesman"?
8. Does the word "person" as used in the Act include within its meaning individuals, firms, co-partnerships, associations and corporations?
9. How many acts as a real estate broker or as a real estate salesman will require a person engaged in such activity to take out a license?
10. Are there any exceptions to the application of the Act?
11. Is it unlawful to carry on or hold one's self out as a real estate broker or salesman without having a license?
12. May cities, counties or towns require a business license fee from real estate brokers and salesmen?
13. Is it possible for a nonresident of the state to procure a license to act as a real estate broker in this state?
14. Is it necessary for a nonresident broker to maintain a place of business within this state?
15. Can a nonresident broker with nonresident license be sued in the state even if he is not actually in this state?
16. Is it possible for a nonresident of the state to procure a license to act as a real estate salesman in this state?
17. Will the applicant for a nonresident salesman's license be required to take a written examination?
18. What is the general nature of the penalty for violating the real estate broker's license act?
19. In case the Act is violated by a corporation or by a partnership, who is subject to the punishment prescribed in the Act?

20. What does the term "Business chance broker" include?

21. Who administers the business chance broker's law?

22. Are business chance brokers subject to the provisions of the real estate broker's license act?

23. In case a real estate salesman desires to change his employer, what must be done?

24. What are the legal requirements for branch offices?

25. Does the law provide the qualification of a manager of a branch office?

KEY (CORRECT ANSWERS)

1. Who are real estate brokers within the meaning of the Act?

   The definition of a real estate broker as contained in the Act is all-inclusive and covers almost every act or service which one, for compensation, or expectation thereof, my perform or render for another, relative to real estate. The term "real estate broker" includes all persons, partnerships, associations and corporations, who, for another and for compensation, or in expectation or upon the promise of receiving or collecting the same, does any of the following things:

   Sells, exchanges, purchases; rents or leases real estate; offers to sell, exchange, purchase, rent or lease real estate; negotiates, or offers or attempts or agrees to negotiate the sale, exchange, purchase, rental or leasing of real estate; lists or offers or attempts or agrees to list real estate for sale; appraises or offers or attempts or agrees to appraise real estate; auctions, or offers or attempts or agrees to auction real estate; buys or sells or offers to buy or sell, or otherwise deals in options on real estate; collects or offers or attempts or agrees to collect rental for the use of real estate; advertises or holds himself out as being engaged in the business of buying, selling, exchanging, renting or leasing real estate; assists or directs in the procuring of prospects, calculated to result in the sale, exchange, leasing or rental of real estate; assists or directs in the negotiation or closing of any transaction calculated or intended to result in the sale, exchange, leasing or rental of real estate.

   The term "real estate broker" also shall mean and include any person employed by or on behalf of the owner or owners of real estate at a stated salary or upon a commission or upon a salary and commission basis or other compensation to sell, exchange or offer for sale such real estate, or any part thereof and who shall sell or exchange, or offer or attempt or agree to negotiate the sale or exchange of any lot or parcel of real estate.

2. What is meant by the word "compensation" as used in the definition of real estate broker?

   The word "compensation" means and includes any fee, commission, salary, money or valuable consideration for services rendered or to be rendered as well as the promise thereof and whether contingent or otherwise.

3. Does the term "valuable consideration" as used in the definition of a real estate broker, mean only a money consideration?

   No. A valuable consideration may consist of property, the rendition of services, the granting of a favor, or anything which the parties themselves or the law deems to be of value; even slight value, will be enough to constitute "valuable consideration."

4. Does the term "real estate" as used in the Act refer only to the land itself, without improvements?

   No. The term "real estate" includes all buildings, fixtures and improvements attached to the land, and includes standing timber.

5. Does one engaged in the business of real property management come within the Act?

   The answer to this question is like splitting a hair. Generally, if in the course of such management he performs one of the acts enumerated in the Act, such as renting or collecting rentals, he would be a real estate broker; however, a recent amendment to the law excludes from the definition of "real estate broker" any person engaged in the management, but not sale, of commercial properties.

6. What is meant by the term "associate real estate broker?"
An associate real estate broker is a person who has qualified as a real estate broker, who works for a designated broker and whose license states he is associated with a designated broker.

7. What is meant by the term "real estate salesman?"
A real estate salesman means any person, who, for compensation or in the expectation or upon the promise thereof, is employed or engaged by a licensed real estate broker to do any act or deals in any transaction listed in the definition of a "real estate broker" for or on behalf of such licensed real estate broker.

8. Does the word "person" as used in the Act include within its meaning individuals, firms, co-partnerships, associations and corporations?
Yes.

9. How many acts as a real estate broker or as a real estate salesman will require a person engaged in such activity to take out a license?
One.

10. Are there any exceptions to the application of the Act?
Yes. It does not apply to attorneys-in-fact who function only for the consummation of a transaction, to attorneys at law while acting as such, or to trustees under a trust agreement; or to those who as owner, lessor, lessee, perform any acts with reference to property owned or leased by him, or any regular employee of any person, partnership, association or corporation who performs any acts with reference to property owned or leased by such person, which are incidental to other principal activities or business of a non-real estate nature of the employer; or any person engaged in the management, but not sale, of commercial properties.

11. Is it unlawful to carry on or hold one's self out as a real estate broker or salesman without having a license?
Yes. The Act prescribes severe penalties for the unlawful practice of real estate.

12. May cities, counties or towns require a business license fee from real estate brokers and salesmen?
No. After the broker or salesman has obtained a license from the real estate division, additional license fees are expressly prohibited by law. (This does not apply to business chance brokers.)

13. Is it possible for a nonresident of the state to procure a license to act as a real estate broker in this state?
Yes. A nonresident, who is a licensed broker in another state, may be licensed upon complying with all of the requirements relative to resident brokers, and provided that his state offers the same privilege to the licensed brokers of this state.

14. Is it necessary for a nonresident broker to maintain a place of business within this state?
No. He must, however, maintain a place of business in the other state.

15. Can a nonresident broker with nonresident license be sued in the state even if he is not actually in this state?
    Yes. When a nonresident broker accepts a license, he automatically authorizes service on the commissioner as his representative in any suit or action which may be commenced against him in the proper court of any county in this state in which cause of action may arise. Service of summons or process made on the real estate commissioner shall have the same valid effect as if served on the nonresident licensee personally.

16. Is it possible for a nonresident of the state to procure a license to act as a real estate salesman in this state?
    Yes. A nonresident of this state may be licensed as a real estate salesman upon complying with all the requirements of the law and with all the provisions and conditions of this chapter relative to resident brokers and salesmen, if he is employed by a real estate broker who has complied with all the requirements of this chapter and is duly licensed as a real estate broker by this state.

17. Will the applicant for a nonresident salesman's license be required to take a written examination?
    No. Not if the applicant has qualified in his own state by a written examination.

18. What is the general nature of the penalty for violating the real estate broker's license act?
    Such violation would be considered a misdemeanor.

19. In case the Act is violated by a corporation or by a partnership, who is subject to the punishment prescribed in the Act?
    The officer, member or agent "who personally shall participate in or be accessory to any violation" of the Act by such corporation or partnership shall be subject to the prescribed penalties.

20. What does the term "Business chance broker" include?
    It includes all persons, firms, corporations, and associations that engage directly or indirectly in the business of buying, selling or dealing in any established business or business opportunity or good will or any interest therein, or who for profit, compensation or commission engage in the business of offering to establish others in business or who declare to the public that they are engaged in the business of buying, selling or dealing in established businesses or business opportunities.

21. Who administers the business chance broker's law?
    The real estate commissioner.

22. Are business chance brokers subject to the provisions of the real estate broker's license act?
    Yes. The Act specifically states that the real estate commissioner shall have power to issue, deny, suspend and revoke licenses in the manner and under the terms and conditions in the real estate law, and they will be governed by the rules and regulations of the real estate board.

23. In case a real estate salesman desires to change his employer, what must be done?

He should obtain from the division a form for real estate salesman's license transfer; request the broker by whom he is employed to send to the commissioner his license (the broker shall do so without delay) and obtain the signature of the broker on the transfer form; go to the broker whose employment he will enter and obtain his signature; mail the completed real estate salesman's license transfer, his pocket card and the fee for transfer of license to the division.

24. What are the legal requirements for branch offices?

Every additional office or place of business other than the principal place of business of a broker shall be licensed only with the approval of the real estate commissioner after the broker has given satisfactory proof that this additional place of business will be so located as to receive the broker's personal supervision, or that it will be under the supervision of a duly licensed competent employee of the broker, approved by the commissioner. Every such office shall be designated a *BRANCH OFFICE by* an appropriate sign displayed in the manner provided by the law.

25. Does the law provide the qualification of a manager of a branch office?

Yes. Each branch office shall be in charge of an associate broker or a licensed salesman with at least two years' experience as a salesman.

TEST 2

DIRECTIONS: In continuous discourse, briefly and concisely answer the following questions.

1. Where a license is issued to a partnership or a corporation, is the person designated to act on behalf of the group authorized by the license to conduct a real estate business in his own name?

2. May a partnership or corporation be represented by members or officers other than the one designated in its application?

3. Can a salesman be a member of a partnership or an officer of a corporation?

4. How does a broker change the name under which he will operate?

5. How is a change made of location of a branch office?

6. What are the requirements of the employer broker upon the termination of the salesman's employment?

7. What is the effect of a salesman's failure to notify the commissioner of a change of employer?

8. How are salesmen affected by a revocation or suspension of the license of their employer broker?

9. What is the effect upon the license of a partnership, or a corporation, of a revocation or suspension of the license issued to the member authorized to act on behalf of the partnership or corporation?

10. Must a broker remove his sign when he moves his office?

11. May a real estate broker who is not a Realtor advertise or hold himself out as such?

12. In case a real estate broker desires to change his place of business, what must he do?

13. Is a real estate broker required to post or erect a sign at his place of business?

14. When a license expires at the end of the license year and an application to renew, together with the fee, is not made until ten days later, is the licensee permitted by law to engage in the real estate business during that ten day period?

15. Is it necessary for a real estate broker or salesman to have his license on his person at all times?

16. Is the licensee furnished with any evidence showing his authority to transact business as a broker or salesman?

17. How many places of business may a real estate broker maintain?

18. Is the broker notified when a salesman in his employ makes application for a broker's license?

19. The manual says a broker "cannot delegate his authority." Does he not do this when he appoints a branch office manager?

20. What is meant by the "Shall Nots"?

KEY (CORRECT ANSWERS)

1. Where a license is issued to a partnership or a corporation, is the person designated to act on behalf of the group authorized by the license to conduct a real estate business in his own name?

    No. If he desires to conduct a real estate business in his own name, he must make a separate application for a license as an individual, pay a separate fee, and secure a separate license.

2. May a partnership or corporation be represented by members or officers other than the one designated in its application?

    Yes. Should other members, *other than the one designated in the application,* desire to act on behalf of the group, each such member is required to take out a separate broker's license and pay the required fees. Such a licensee is not authorized to transact real estate business in his own name.

3. Can a salesman be a member of a partnership or an officer of a corporation?

    No. The law provides that every member of a partnership or officer of a corporation who will perform any of the acts constituting the practice of real estate shall be licensed as a broker.

4. How does a broker change the name under which he will operate?

    Get from the division, a form known as request for real estate broker's change of name; complete the form and return to the division with his license and pocket card, the licenses and pocket cards of his salesmen; and fees for himself and for each salesman.

5. How is a change made of location of a branch office?

    Obtain from the division, the form for request for real estate broker's branch office; complete and return to the division with the fee. A branch office license is not transferable.

6. What are the requirements of the employer broker upon the termination of the salesman's employment?

    The employer-broker shall immediately return the salesman's license to the division for cancellation. The broker shall, at the time of returning the salesman's license, notify the salesman at his last known address of the return of his license to the commissioner. A copy of such communication to the salesman shall accompany the license when mailed or delivered to the commissioner.

7. What is the effect of a salesman's failure to notify the commissioner of a change of employer?

    Failure to notify the commissioner within ten days automatically cancels the salesman's license.

8. How are salesmen affected by a revocation or suspension of the license of their employer broker?

    Their licenses are immediately and automatically suspended pending a change of employer and a transfer of license. Should any of the salesmen enter the employ of another broker during the same year, a new license will be issued to the salesman without charge upon the surrender of his former license and pocket card.

9. What is the effect upon the license of a partnership, or a corporation, of a revocation or suspension of the license issued to the member authorized to act on behalf of the partnership or corporation?

The license of the partnership or corporation shall be revoked unless, within a time to be fixed by the commissioner, the offending member is discharged.

10. Must a broker remove his sign when he moves his office?

Yes.

11. May a real estate broker who is not a Realtor advertise or hold himself out as such?

No. The word is in effect a coined term and may only be used under certain conditions. Its unauthorized use may be enjoined by the courts and such a use is ground for revocation of a license.

12. In case a real estate broker desires to change his place of business, what must he do?

He must notify the commissioner on a form supplied by the division; send in his license and pocket card and the licenses and pocket cards of all salesmen in his employ; and remit for the reissuance of his license and for reissuance of each salesman's license.

13. Is a real estate broker required to post or erect a sign at his place of business?

Yes. Each place of business must be designated by a sign containing the name under which the broker is licensed, together with the words "Real Estate," or if a member of the National Association of Real Estate Boards, the word "Realtor." Each sign shall be written in letters not less than one inch in height and placed so that it can be easily observed and read by anyone entering the place of business.

14. When a license expires at the end of the license year and an application to renew, together with the fee, is not made until ten days later, is the licensee permitted by law to engage in the real estate business during that ten day period?

No. The license is automatically suspended until the fee is paid. In such an instance the licensee was unlawfully engaged in real estate, and could be required to take another examination.

15. Is it necessary for a real estate broker or salesman to have his license on his person at all times?

No. All licenses are in the custody and control of the broker and must be displayed at his principal place of business.

16. Is the licensee furnished with any evidence showing his authority to transact business as a broker or salesman?

Yes. Pocket cards are furnished by the Commissioner for that purpose.

17. How many places of business may a real estate broker maintain?

At least one is required. He may maintain as many branch offices as he desires so long as they comply with the law. Each place of business must be registered with the real estate division and an annual fee is paid to cover each branch office licensed.

18. Is the broker notified when a salesman in his employ makes application for a broker's license?

Yes. The applicant is obliged to have the broker complete the form for verification of salesman experience claim by employer broker.

19. The manual says a broker "cannot delegate his authority." Does he not do this when he appoints a branch office manager?

Under the law of agency a broker cannot transfer the legal rights his principal has against him. In appointing a branch office manager he is merely delegating limited responsibilities to the manager. It should also be kept in mind that this delegation does not mean abdication by the broker. A recent court decision stated "a salesman is strictly an employee of the broker. He should not collect money from customers or actively-take charge of the broker's office".

20. What is meant by the "Shall Nots"?

Sufficient cause for the suspension or revocation of a license would be proof of any of the following:
1. Making any substantial misrepresentations.
2. Making false promises.
3. Unauthorized use of the word "Realtor."
4. Representing both parties to a transaction without the knowledge of both.
5. If a salesman, accepting compensation from one not his employer.
6. If a salesman, representing another broker without his employer's consent.
7. Failing to account for another's money or other property within a reasonable time.

EXAMINATION SECTION
TEST 1

DIRECTIONS: Each question or incomplete statement is followed by several suggested answers or completions. Select the one that *BEST* answers the question or completes the statement. *PRINT THE LETTER OF THE CORRECT ANSWER IN THE SPACE AT THE RIGHT.*

1. What is the purpose of state regulation of real estate salesmen and brokers? 1.____

    A. To insure that all brokers and salesmen have the same or equivalent credentials.
    B. To make certain that the state has a record of everyone in this profession.
    C. To protect dealers in real estate from unlicensed persons who act as brokers and to protect the public from inept or dishonest persons.
    D. To make it easier for real estate to be sold.

2. Which of the following is *NOT* a proper subject for a real estate salesman to handle? 2.____

    A. A burial plot
    B. A mortgage
    C. The rental on a summer cottage
    D. The collection of rent

3. The state regulates the real estate profession by authority of 3.____

    A. its interest in the land
    B. eminent domain
    C. its police power
    D. its taxing power

4. "Real estate," as used in the profession, means 4.____

    A. only interests in the land
    B. only fee simple interests
    C. tenements
    D. tenements, hereditaments, and all interests in land

5. Which of the following is a real estate broker? 5.____

    A. A real estate gallery which lists property and secures a fee for such listings
    B. A broker who negotiates the purchase and sale of bonds and other securities based upon real estate mortgages but who does not negotiate the loan which gives rise to the security
    C. A janitor or superintendent who collects rents and is employed by the owner of the building
    D. All of the above

6. A person, co-partnership, or corporation can engage in or hold itself out as a real estate broker or salesman 6.____

    A. at all times provided there is no sale if not licensed
    B. at all times when an application for a license is pending
    C. As long as his employer or partner has a license
    D. only if he, himself, is licensed

7. A real estate broker must be

   A. 21 years old to be eligible for a license
   B. 18 years old to be eligible for a license
   C. a high school graduate
   D. a college graduate

8. A real estate salesman must be

   A. 21 years old to be eligible for a license
   B. 18 years old to be eligible for a license
   C. a high school graduate
   D. a college graduate

9. A real estate broker must

   A. be a United States citizen to be licensed
   B. have declared his intention of becoming a citizen of the United States
   C. have declared his intention of becoming a United States citizen and actually have become one within 7 years or suffer revocation of his license or refusal to renew
   D. be a resident of the United States for 10 years

10. A broker's or salesman's license will NOT be given to a person

    A. who has been convicted of a felony anywhere in the United States
    B. who has been convicted of a felony in the licensing state only
    C. who has been convicted of a felony anywhere in the United States and if such offense is cognizable as a felony in the licensing state as well
    D. none of the above

11. A person who has been convicted of a felony so as to be ineligible for a broker's or salesman's license

    A. may never get a license
    B. must wait ten years to be eligible
    C. must petition the state licensing board to be eligible
    D. will be eligible subsequent to conviction if he has received an executive pardon or a certificate of good conduct from a parole board

12. An application for a broker's license would MOST surely be turned down if the Division of Licenses in the Department of State believed that

    A. the applicant could not write well in English
    B. the applicant is untrustworthy
    C. the applicant did not graduate from college
    D. the applicant was never a real estate salesman

13. Which of the following is NOT a mandatory requirement for an applicant for a broker's license?

    A. Knowledge of the English language
    B. Knowledge of deeds, mortgages, land contracts of sale, leases
    C. Experience as a licensed real estate salesman for at least two years
    D. A determination of the applicant's trustworthy nature

14. Which of the following is NOT an alternative qualification for obtaining a broker's license? 14._____

    A. Active participation in the real estate brokerage business as a licensed salesman for 2 years
    B. General experience in brokerage business for 2 years
    C. Active participation in general real estate brokerage business as a licensed salesman for at least one year and attendance for at least 45 hours on a real estate course approved by the Secretary of State
    D. A voucher by a real estate broker that the applicant is competent in this field

15. Legal title to real estate passes when 15._____

    A. a duly executed deed is delivered to the buyer
    B. the deed is properly signed
    C. the deed is notarized and sealed
    D. the deed is recorded

16. In order to accurately ascertain the CORRECT boundaries of real property, one should obtain a(n) 16._____

    A. title policy
    B. survey
    C. abstract
    D. warranty deed

17. The person who conveys title to real estate is called the 17._____

    A. grantee
    B. trustee
    C. grantor
    D. executor

18. Title to real estate is conveyed when 18._____

    A. the act of sale is recorded
    B. the act of sale is signed by the parties
    C. copy of the act of sale is received
    D. parties agree to sell to buyer

19. Title to fixtures, shelves, counters and merchandise is transferred or conveyed by if the 19._____

    A. deed
    B. bill of sale
    C. security agreement
    D. escrow

20. The rights of a person who owns a property but has leased it to someone else are referred to as _____ estate. 20._____

    A. lessee's
    B. fee simple
    C. leasehold
    D. leased fee

21. Untrue statements made on an application for either a broker's or salesman's license

    A. must be corrected within 30 days
    B. don't matter since the department will check each answer any way
    C. will be punished by taking away the license
    D. will be adjudged as perjury and treated as such

22. All of the following statements about deeds are true EXCEPT:

    A. A deed must be in writing
    B. Delivery of a deed takes place whether or not the physical paper leaves the possession of the grantor
    C. If the grantor gives the deed to the grantee, a valid delivery has been executed, regardless of the intention of the grantor
    D. A deed is duly executed when it is signed and intended to operate as such by the grantor

23. An applicant who does NOT apply for renewal within the specified time

    A. may never receive a renewal
    B. may ask for special dispensation upon appropriate grounds
    C. may qualify by taking the written examination
    D. receives a renewal as a matter of right

24. The license of a real estate salesman is kept by

    A. the license department
    B. the salesman
    C. the broker who employs the salesman
    D. all of the above

25. If a salesman voluntarily leaves his job,

    A. the salesman's license must be returned to the department
    B. the salesman must take the license with him to his next employer
    C. the former employer must keep the license on file for one year
    D. the salesman must get a photostat of his license to take with him

KEY (CORRECT ANSWERS)

1.	C	11.	D
2.	A	12.	B
3.	C	13.	C
4.	D	14.	D
5.	A	15.	A
6.	D	16.	B
7.	A	17.	C
8.	B	18.	B
9.	C	19.	A
10.	C	20.	D

21. D
22. C
23. C
24. C
25. A

TEST 2

DIRECTIONS: Each question or incomplete statement is followed by several suggested answers or completions. Select the one that BEST answers the question or completes the statement. PRINT THE LETTER OF THE CORRECT ANSWER IN THE SPACE AT THE RIGHT.

1. After a salesman has voluntarily left his job for another company and his employer returns his license to the department,

    A. the salesman must requalify for the license
    B. the department will forthwith re-issue the license
    C. the salesman must pay $1 and submit written notification of new employment to have his license re-issued
    D. The salesman need only submit the name and address of his new employer-broker

2. A purchaser of real property, all other things being equal, would prefer to have a

    A. warranty deed
    B. quitclaim deed
    C. bargain and sale deed without covenant against grantor
    D. referee's deed

3. Which of the following is a FALSE statement?

    A. Each licensed broker shall have and maintain a definite place of business within the state.
    B. Each licensed broker shall conspicuously post on the outside of the building or in some other suitable place the words "licensed real estate broker."
    C. Each licensed broker shall be required to display his license only in his main office, not in his branch offices.
    D. Each licensed broker shall display as many licenses as he has officers.

4. Licenses issued to real estate brokers

    A. must be conspicuously displayed
    B. must be available upon request
    C. must be on file with company records
    D. must be put on the front door of each office

5. A change in business address by a licensee

    A. must be inserted in colored ink on the license by the licensee
    B. is to be ignored until the licensee applies for a renewal of his license
    C. must be telephoned to the department of licenses for its records
    D. must be given to the department in writing, whereupon the department shall issue a new license upon return of the original license and pocket card and payment

6. A change in address by a licensee without notification and re-issue

    A. makes the licensee guilty of perjury
    B. annuls the license
    C. makes the licensee ineligible for renewal
    D. has no legal effect

7. A pocket card shall be issued by the department to each licensed broker or salesman

   A. on demand
   B. on payment of a fee
   C. as a matter of law
   D. in special cases

8. A pocket card is

   A. like a business card
   B. an evidence of insurance
   C. like a certificate
   D. is an extra used to impress clients

9. The pocket card

   A. must be prominently displayed by the broker or salesman at all times
   B. must be kept with company records
   C. must be given to each client
   D. must be shown on demand

10. A warranty deed

    A. must be specified in the contract for sale of the property
    B. is assumed if no type of deed is specified
    C. is an option open to the grantee after the contract is closed
    D. is an extraordinary type of deed

11. In terms of a deed, the grantee is the

    A. title company
    B. buyer
    C. broker
    D. seller

12. The re-issuance of a license

    A. requires a new certificate to be issued
    B. permits the department to endorse a license and pocket card previously issued
    C. requires that the department state in a conspicuous place on the certificate how many renewals have been made
    D. requires none of the above

13. The death of a real estate broker who was at the time of his death the sole proprietor of a brokerage office

    A. revokes the broker's license as of the date of death
    B. has no effect on the others in the office
    C. permits the decedent's administrator or executor to complete any unfinished transactions for a 120-day period
    D. gives all salesmen and the decedent's administrator 120 days to transact new, as well as complete unfinished, business

14. Which of the following is a good information resource for those seeking information about abutters to a property?

    A. Registry of probate
    B. Registry of deeds
    C. Genealogical library
    D. Town assessor's office

15. The *riparian doctrine* in real estate is concerned with

    A. the government's right to take possession of property
    B. water rights
    C. land boundary settlement
    D. proximity to the nearest running stream or river

16. The information in most older recorded deeds, including names and signatures, comprises

    A. originals   B. abstracts   C. transcriptions   D. extracts

17. Which of the following is a term used for an adjoining neighbor in many deed records?

    A. Associate   B. Abstracter   C. Adjacent   D. Abutter

18. A broker's license issued to a corporation entitles

    A. all officers of the corporation to act as a real estate broker
    B. only the secretary of the corporation to act as a real estate broker
    C. only the president to act as a real estate broker
    D. none of the above

19. A member of a co-partnership or corporation licensed as a real estate broker

    A. does not have to pay an additional license fee for his license if he is not the president of the corporation
    B. cannot get a real estate salesman's license
    C. can always apply for a real estate salesman's license
    D. pays only half as much as the corporation or co-partnership for his license

20. An individual real estate broker who becomes an officer of a corporation

    A. may have his license endorsed by the department so that he may act as the corporation's representative
    B. must pay for a new license but does not have to take the test again
    C. must wait for the term of his license to expire before the corporation applies for a license for him
    D. may have his license endorsed by the board of directors so that he may act as the corporation's representative

21. What is the specific term for the conveyance of a future interest in real property by the person holding that interest to the person holding the prior possessory interest?

    A. Reversion   B. Surrender   C. Remainder   D. Release

22. Which of the following is grounds for suspension or revocation by the department of state of a broker's license?

    A. Conviction of violation of a rule
    B. Material misstatement in the application for a license
    C. Incompetency
    D. All of the above

23. After a broker's license has been revoked or suspended, which of these circumstances may result?
    1. The license may be displayed pending an appeal.
    2. The license must not be displayed.
    3. The license must be returned to the department of state.
    4. The license may be held in escrow by an attorney or a bank.

    The CORRECT combination is:

    A. 1, 3   B. 2, 4   C. 1, 4   D. 2, 3

24. When a broker's or salesman's license is revoked by the department, the broker or salesman   24.____

    A. can never be re-licensed
    B. must petition the department within 6 months to be relicensed
    C. cannot be relicensed until after the expiration of one year
    D. cannot be relicensed until after the expiration of five years

25. How can a broker's "untrustworthiness" be shown? By   25.____

    A. proof of racial discrimination in renting or selling
    B. proof of placement of "blind ads"
    C. failure to indicate "dealer" in an advertisement
    D. all of the above

KEY (CORRECT ANSWERS)

1.	C	11.	B
2.	A	12.	B
3.	C	13.	C
4.	A	14.	D
5.	D	15.	B
6.	B	16.	C
7.	C	17.	D
8.	B	18.	C
9.	D	19.	B
10.	A	20.	A

21.	D
22.	D
23.	D
24.	C
25.	D

TEST 3

DIRECTIONS: Each question or incomplete statement is followed by several suggested answers or completions. Select the one that BEST answers the question or completes the statement. PRINT THE LETTER OF THE CORRECT ANSWER IN THE SPACE AT THE RIGHT.

1. The revocation of a broker's license

    A. has no effect on the validity of the licenses of his salesmen
    B. has no effect on the validity of the licenses of his salesmen if they find new employment with a licensed broker within one month
    C. suspends the licenses of his salesmen until they find new employment and get new licenses
    D. revokes the licenses of his salesmen as well

2. If his employer-broker license has been revoked,

    A. the salesman-employee must pay for a new license in order to work for a new, employer
    B. the salesman-employee will be issued a new license without charge
    C. the samesman-employee must only pay half the cost of the original license
    D. none of the above, or all of the above

3. The department of state, before denying an application for license or before revoking or suspending any license or imposing any find or reprimand on the holder,

    A. shall call the applicant or licensee and tell him of the charges against him
    B. shall subpoena the applicant or licensee to appear
    C. shall notify in writing the applicant or licensee of the charges against him at least 20 days prior to the date set for hearing
    D. none of the above, or all of the above

4. At a hearing to determine whether a license should be revoked or an application denied,

    A. the applicant or licensee must appear in person
    B. the applicant or licensee must be represented by counsel
    C. the applicant or licensee must appear with counsel
    D. the applicant or licensee has a choice whether to appear in person or be represented by counsel

5. Which of the following concerning the notice of the charges and the hearing are TRUE? It
    1. may be served by delivery to the applicant or licensee
    2. may be served by registered mail to the last known business address of the licensee
    3. shall also be given to the broker-employer if the charges are against a salesman
    4. shall be contained in a subpoena and served personally on the licensee

    The CORRECT combination is:

    A. 1, 2   B. 4 only   C. 1, 2, 3   D. 1, 2, 3, 4

6. The department   6._____

    A. can suspend a license pending a hearing
    B. cannot suspend a license until the hearing has ascertained the licensee's guilt
    C. can hold the licensee in contempt until it has determined his innocence or guilt
    D. has a choice of any one of the above alternatives

7. What is the term for land rights based on occupation, rather than conveyance?   7._____

    A. Adverse claim
    B. Domain
    C. Easement appurtenant
    D. Indentured jurisdiction

8. The granting or the refusal to grant a license or renewal and the imposition of a fine or reprimand or the refusal to impose a fine or reprimand   8._____

    A. is final
    B. is subject to the review of the courts
    C. is subject to review by the Attorney General
    D. can only be questioned by the license holder or applicant

9. Which of the following is a *TRUE* statement?   9._____

    A. A broker may never split a commission with another broker.
    B. A broker cannot split a commission with a broker from another state.
    C. A broker can split his commission with whoever deserves a part thereof.
    D. A broker can split his commission with a licensed salesman

10. A broker *CANNOT*   10._____

    A. split his commission with a broker from another state
    B. split his commission with a party to the transaction
    C. split his commission with a licensed salesman
    D. split his commission

11. Which of the following is *FALSE*?   11._____

    A. A real estate broker cannot offer prizes for names of prospective customers.
    B. Payment for names of prospective customers does not violate a rule.
    C. An unlicensed broker cannot recover a fee for his aid from a licensed broker.
    D. A broker may share a commission with a broker licensed in another state although he is not licensed in this state.

12. A real estate salesman   12._____

    A. may be paid only by his employer
    B. may demand a fee from the party for whom he negotiated the transaction in lieu of his commission due from his employer
    C. may get both a fee from the interested party and from his employer
    D. may get a fee for appraising real estate

13. When a broker discharges a salesman,   13._____

A. the broker must send the salesman's license to the department of state with a sworn statement as to the reason why the salesman was discharged
B. the broker need not report the discharge since the salesman's new employer must report the salesman as a new employee
C. the salesman must send his license in to the department of state
D. the department will ascertain the salesman's new position during its annual investigation of broker's offices

14. When a broker discharges a salesman, 14.___

    A. the salesman will not find out about it until the department of state notifies him
    B. the broker must verbally make it clear to the salesman why he was discharged
    C. the broker must mail the salesman a communication that his license has been returned and a copy of that communication must be attached to the salesman's license when it is returned
    D. the salesman must verify to the department that he had notice from his broker that his license had been returned

15. When the salesman's employment is mutually terminated or he voluntarily terminates his own employment, 15.___

    A. the salesman shall return his license to the department
    B. the salesman shall write to the department the reason why he left the broker's employ
    C. the broker shall send the salesman's license to the department with the reason for the termination of employment attached
    D. none of the above

16. Upon termination of the salesman's employment, 16.___

    A. the broker must send his own license to the department along with that of the salesman
    B. the broker must send his pocket card to the department
    C. the salesman must send his license to the department
    D. the salesman must send his pocket card to the department

17. A real estate salesman may work for a new employer 17.___

    A. immediately, pending the issuance of a new license
    B. immediately, but cannot get a commission until he gets his license
    C. only after the employer gets his license from the department
    D. only if the salesman agrees to his commissions being held in escrow until he gets his license

18. A broker 18.___

    A. bears the responsibility for any wrongdoing of his employees
    B. bears the responsibility for only those acts of his employees done in the course of their employment
    C. can have his license suspended or revoked if he knows that his employee has committed a wrongdoing or keeps the profits thereof
    D. is not responsible for any wrongdoing of his employees unless he, himself, took an active part therein

19. If an unlicensed salesman or a salesman without a temporary permit works for a licensed broker,   19._____

    A. the salesman is guilty of a misdemeanor
    B. the broker is guilty of a misdemeanor
    C. the salesman is guilty of a felony
    D. the salesman can work until he gets his license

20. In order to bring or maintain a court action for compensation for services rendered,   20._____

    A. a salesman or broker must prove his part in the transaction
    B. a salesman or broker must state and prove that he was duly licensed on the date the action allegedly arose
    C. a salesman or broker must prove that he is duly licensed on the date of trial
    D. the defendant must prove that the salesman or broker was not licensed on the date of the action

21. Which of the following is *FALSE?*   21._____

    A. A transaction by an unlicensed broker is unlawful and an assignee acquires no enforceable rights under such contract to pay commission.
    B. Where only one of two co-brokers engaged in the sale or lease of property is duly licensed, neither broker is entitled to recover for his services.
    C. A real estate broker is entitled to a commission arising from the sale of real estate where he was not a licensed broker at the time he obtained a purchaser since he was not to be paid his commission until title had passed and since he had obtained his license between the time he procured the purchaser and the time title passed.
    D. Commissions lawfully earned by a duly licensed real estate salesman do not cease to be payable to him by reason of a change in his employment before he has received same.

22. A violation of any provision of a rule is a   22._____

    A. misdemeanor
    B. felony
    C. misdemeanor or felony depending upon which provision is violated
    D. perjury

23. The highest form of an estate, under which the owner can use the property at will and depose of it without restriction, is   23._____

    A. leasehold
    B. fee simple
    C. leased fee
    D. life estate

24. A violation of a provision is committed when   24._____

    A. the intent of the provision is defied
    B. a single act which is prohibited is committed
    C. someone is hurt by the commission of the prohibited act
    D. a series of wrongful deeds produces an unjust enrichment for the broker

25. Ideally, a title chain developed during a search should go back at least to the

    A. very first owner of the parcel
    B. developer of the subdivision
    C. first owner after the initial subdivision
    D. last known owner

KEY (CORRECT ANSWERS)

1. C
2. B
3. C
4. D
5. C

6. A
7. A
8. B
9. D
10. B

11. A
12. A
13. A
14. C
15. C

16. D
17. C
18. C
19. B
20. B

21. C
22. A
23. B
24. B
25. B

TEST 4

DIRECTIONS: Each question or incomplete statement is followed by several suggested answers or completions. Select the one that *BEST* answers the question or completes the statement. *PRINT THE LETTER OF THE CORRECT ANSWER IN THE SPACE AT THE RIGHT.*

1. An offender who has received any sum of money as commission, compensation, or profit as a consequence of his violation 1.____

    A. shall be liable for exactly the amount he wrongly received
    B. shall be liable for not more than half the amount he wrongly received
    C. shall be held liable for four times the amount he wrongly received
    D. may be held liable up to four times the amount he wrongly received

2. What is the term for the voluntary conveyance of title to land from an individual private owner to a public agency? 2.____

    A. Dedication
    B. Accretion
    C. Escheat
    D. Accession

3. Which of the following statements is TRUE regarding both liens and easements? They 3.____

    A. must be recorded in public land records to be legal
    B. are both encumbrances
    C. may be imposed against the property only after all parties involved have agreed
    D. must be in writing to be legal

4. What is the term for an improvement or object, such as a building or driveway, that extends across the legal boundary of an adjoining tract of land? 4.____

    A. Lien
    B. Encroachment
    C. Encumbrance
    D. Easement

5. In a prosecution for a wrong allegedly done by a real estate broker, 5.____

    A. the broker must prove beyond a shadow of a doubt that the other party agreed to pay him the commission he was given
    B. the aggrieved party must allege and prove that there was an agreement to pay the broker but it was bad
    C. it is presumed that any broker who offers to negotiate a sale of real estate for another is doing so for a fee
    D. none of the above

6. A real estate transaction is presumed to be done for a commission 6.____

    A. whenever one goes to a broker for his professional advice
    B. whenever a broker completes a transaction which benefits a private
    C. whenever the broker performs repeated and successive acts, offers or attempts, and can prove the same
    D. all of the above

7. Who has the power to enforce the provisions of licensing statutes?

   A. Secretary of State
   B. Attorney General
   C. District Attorney
   D. All of the above

8. Violations of licensing statutes and rules

   A. are investigated on complaint of any person
   B. are investigated on the initiative of the officer in charge
   C. are investigated on the initiative of the officer in charge and/or on the complaint of any person
   D. are investigated by the Grand Jury

9. The investigative powers

   A. are limited to the alleged violations
   B. extend to the alleged violations, business practices and methods of the company
   C. extend to the alleged violations, business practices and methods of the company, and any other related item within the discretion of the investigating officer
   D. are limited by the warrant used by the officer

10. The investigation

    A. is limited to the pertinent data surrounding the alleged violation
    B. is all-inclusive, and any information must be supplied on request by the licensee
    C. does not permit the investigatory officer to ask personal or non-business questions, since this is a violation of the First Amendment
    D. none of the above

11. A person under investigation

    A. can be subpoenaed to appear
    B. must be given a month's notice of the date of his appearance
    C. can only be subpoenaed if he is the owner of the business
    D. can be subpoenaed only if he is to appear in his own county

12. A person under investigation

    A. is under oath when he gives testimony
    B. is not under oath when he gives testimony since this is not a court of law
    C. is on his honor to tell the truth
    D. none of the above

13. A person who does NOT appear when subpoenaed

    A. suffers no penalty if he comes the second time
    B. is given 30 days to defend himself
    C. is guilty of a misdemeanor
    D. may be guilty of a misdemeanor if he has no valid excuse

14. A person who refuses to answer a question when his deposition is being taken

    A. is guilty of a misdemeanor
    B. is guilty of a misdemeanor depending upon the question

C. is guilty of a misdemeanor if he has no valid reason for not answering
D. is guilty of a violation of the Fifth Amendment

15. During an investigation for alleged violation,

   A. the person must answer each and every question at his peril at all times
   B. the person being investigated can be given an immunity from prosecution by the presiding official if he answers questions put to him which may incriminate him
   C. the person being investigated must be given immunity before he can answer any questions
   D. the person being investigated is only entitled to be given an immunity if he is in criminal court

16. Which of the following statements is *FALSE?*

   A. An attorney at law is not required to be licensed in order to act as a real estate broker.
   B. An attorney who is not licensed as a real estate broker may act as co-broker with a licensed real estate broker and share the brokerage compensation.
   C. Salesmen employed by an attorney who acts as a real estate broker do not have to be licensed.
   D. Any public officer or a person acting under court order does not have to be licensed to act as a real estate broker.

17. An attorney who deals exclusively in real estate

   A. must have a real estate broker's license
   B. does not need a license
   C. can recover the commission for someone who is unlicensed as an assignee
   D. and has a license can no longer act as a broker if his license is revoked

18. A non-resident real estate broker

   A. shall be required to maintain a place of business in this state
   B. must maintain a place of business in this state if he does not maintain a definite place of business in another state
   C. cannot act as a real estate broker in this state unless he is licensed by this state
   D. is not required to maintain a place of business in this state regardless of whether or not he has a definite place of business in another state

19. A non-resident real estate broker

   A. must take the examination and obtain a license to act in this state
   B. can act in this state without a license
   C. only needs a license to act in this state if his own state requires licensed non-residents to get a license in that state
   D. does not need a license although his resident state requires non-residents to get a state license

20. If the non-resident is licensed in another state but that state does not require a written examination,

    A. he must pay the license fee to get a license from this state
    B. he must pay the license fee and submit a certified copy of the non-state license to get a license from this state
    C. he must take this state's written examination, pay the license fee and submit a copy of his license to get a license from this state
    D. he does not have to do anything to get a license from this state other than submit a copy of his non-state license

21. Every non-resident, upon filing an application for a license or renewal,

    A. shall state his address and main place of business
    B. shall file an irrevocable consent to be sued in this state by submitting himself to the jurisdiction of the state courts
    C. waives the right to be sued in this state
    D. retains the right to be sued in his home state and cannot be sued in any other state

22. In a suit by a resident against a non-resident real estate broker,

    A. the plaintiff must hire a deputy to personally serve the non-resident when he is in the plaintiff's state
    B. the plaintiff must hire a deputy to personally serve the non-resident in his home state
    C. the plaintiff can either serve the secretary of state personally or by registered mail, and must enclose a specified fee
    D. the plaintiff must serve the secretary of state personally and must enclose a fee

23. How is a non-resident broker or salesman notified of a suit against him? By

    A. personal service of process by the plaintiff when he is in the plaintiff's state
    B. registered mail from the plaintiff to the non-resident's out-of-state office
    C. notification from the department of state
    D. registered mail from the secretary of state of the plaintiff's state

24. Each non-resident broker or salesman

    A. must carry his home state's pocket card to show on request in this state
    B. must carry a pocket card issued by the department of state of this state which is distinguishable from that of resident brokers and salesmen
    C. must carry a pocket card issued by the department of state of this state which is a different color than that of resident brokers and salesmen
    D. does not have to carry a pocket card since he is not a resident of this state

25. Which of the following statements is *FALSE?*

    A. The secretary of state can appoint five brokers and five salesmen to an advisory committee to help the department to administer and enforce this article.
    B. The department of state enforces rules.
    C. The advisory committee serves without compensation.
    D. The employees of the department of state who handle real estate affairs are payed according to the civil service law.

KEY (CORRECT ANSWERS)

1.	D	11.	A
2.	A	12.	A
3.	B	13.	D
4.	B	14.	C
5.	C	15.	B
6.	C	16.	C
7.	A	17.	A
8.	C	18.	B
9.	C	19.	C
10.	B	20.	C

21. B
22. C
23. D
24. C
25. A

TEST 5

DIRECTIONS: Each question or incomplete statement is followed by several suggested answers or completions. Select the one that *BEST* answers the question or completes the statement. *PRINT THE LETTER OF THE CORRECT ANSWER IN THE SPACE AT THE RIGHT.*

1. Which combination of the following statements is *FALSE*?
   1. The real estate commission may, on its own motion, investigate any action of a licensee and call the matter for a hearing.
   2. The real estate commission may revoke a broker's license as well as a salesman's license if the salesman is found guilty of conduct of fraudulent or dishonest dealing.
   3. A friend of a broker, not in any way connected with the real estate business, may receive a bonus or a gift, as long as it is not a stated or computed commission, for assisting in making a deal.
   4. A person who was licensed five years ago and has been inactive for two years may, upon application, secure a license for the current year without taking an examination.

   The *CORRECT* combination is:

   A. 1, 2, 3, 4   B. 3, 4   C. 1, 4   D. 2, 4

2. Which combination of the following statements is *FALSE*?
   1. A real estate broker should keep his license in a safety deposit vault or other safe place so that it cannot be lost or stolen.
   2. A salesman may split a commission with any other licensed salesman or broker.
   3. It is lawful for a salesman to complete a deal, collect the commission in his own name, and then give his broker his agreed share.
   4. A real estate salesman can collect, in his own name, money in connection with a real estate transaction.

   The *CORRECT* combination is:

   A. none of the above   B. all of the above
   C. 2, 3, 4   D. 4 only

3. Which combination of the following statements is *TRUE*?
   1. A broker is required to notify the Real Estate Commission immediately after a salesman leaves his employ.
   2. It is not a violation of law for a broker to pay a commission directly to a salesman employed by another broker.
   3. It is a violation of the real estate license law for a salesman or broker to offer as an inducement to enter into a contract for the purchase or sale of real estate anything of value other than the consideration recited in the sales contract.
   4. A real estate broker must notify the real estate commission in writing immediately upon receipt of notice from the surety that the surety has made payment on the broker's bond.

   The *CORRECT* combination is:

   A. 1, 3, 4   B. 1, 3   C. 3, 4   D. 1, 2, 3, 4

4. Which combination of the following statements is *FALSE*?
   1. A broker must immediately notify the real estate commission when he changes his business address.
   2. The owner of a business lot sold it at a figure approximately twice its cost. In showing the adjoining lot to a prospective buyer, a real estate broker is entirely within his rights to make a definite promise of a similar profit to his customer.
   3. A salesman may not sue anyone except his broker for the collection of a real estate commission.
   4. A licensed salesman may divide his commission with another licensed salesman with a broker's consent.

   The *CORRECT* combination is:

   A. 1, 2   B. 2, 3, 4   C. 1, 2, 3, 4   D. 3, 4

5. Which combination of the following statements is *TRUE*?
   1. A person who sells a parcel of real estate under a court order is not required to have a license.
   2. Assessments are for the support of the Government.
   3. Escrow is another name for a husband's interest in his wife's property.
   4. The real estate commission may refuse to issue, revoke, or suspend a license immediately upon receiving a serious complaint against a broker or salesman.

   The *CORRECT* combination is:

   A. 1, 4   B. 1, 2   C. 2 only   D. 1 only

6. Which combination of the following statements is *FALSE*?
   1. A broker who knows that misrepresentations are being made by his salesmen may have his license revoked, even though he, himself, is not guilty of making any misrepresentations.
   2. A broker accepting a net listing to sell a piece of real estate should not accept any compensation from the purchaser unless he reveals this fact to the seller.
   3. It is not necessary for a person to hold a real estate license to execute, buy, or sell an option.
   4. A broker may sell his own personal property to a client without disclosing that fact.

   The *CORRECT* combination is:

   A. 3, 4   B. 1, 4   C. 2, 3   D. 1, 2, 3

7. Which combination of the following statements is *TRUE*?
   1. An applicant for a salesman's license must be a citizen of the United States.
   2. Complete and accurate records of real estate transactions need not be kept by the broker, if the deal is satisfactorily closed.
   3. The salesman should open a separate account for the deposits he receives.
   4. A salesman must include the name of his broker in his advertisements.

   The *CORRECT* combination is:

   A. 1, 2, 4   B. 1, 4   C. 2, 4   D. 1, 3, 4

8. Which combination of the following statements is *FALSE*?
   1. It is necessary that a licensed real estate broker shall erect a sign where he has his office on which shall be plainly stated that he is a licensed real estate broker.
   2. Either the salesman or the broker must witness the contract.
   3. A broker must be the procuring cause to be entitled to a commission on an open listing.
   4. Revocation of the broker's license automatically suspends the salesman's license.
   The *CORRECT* combination is:
   A. 1, 2   B. 3, 4   C. 2 only   D. 2, 4

9. Which combination of the following statements is *FALSE*?
   1. The filing of an application for a license allows the applicant to operate.
   2. If you, a salesman for Broker A, with your Broker's consent, make a deal with Broker B, then, Broker B, knowing you are licensed, can pay you your earned portion of the commission.
   3. If a broker thinks there will be future profits from the resale of property he is selling, he may so guarantee them to his client.
   4. A licensed salesman may go to work for another broker immediately upon the filing of a request for transfer.
   The *CORRECT* combination is:
   A. 1, 3, 4   B. 1, 2, 3, 4   C. 1, 4   D. 3, 4

10. Which combination of the following statements is *FALSE*?
    1. Each branch office of a broker must be in the charge of a licensed broker or salesman.
    2. All listings secured by a salesman belong to the broker.
    3. A real estate salesman should carry his license at all times to properly identify himself.
    4. A real estate salesman must turn all deposits over to his broker.
    The *CORRECT* combination is:
    A. 1, 3   B. 3, 4   C. 1, 3, 4   D. 3 only

11. Which combination of the following statements is *TRUE*?
    1. One real estate transaction requires a license.
    2. The real estate commission has the power to subpoena records in real estate transactions.
    3. Failure to give a buyer a copy of the offer he signs is reason for the revocation of a real estate license.
    4. An employee who only solicits listings need not be licensed.
    The *CORRECT* combination is:
    A. 1, 2   B. 1, 2, 3   C. 2, 3, 4   D. 1, 3, 4

4 (#5)

12. What is the purpose of the law governing real estate brokers and salesmen?
    1. To define the business of real estate brokers and real estate salesmen.
    2. To regulate and supervise the activities of all those engaged in the real estate business as brokers and salesmen.
    3. To require those engaged in such business to have licenses.
    4. To provide methods for the issuance, revocation, and suspension of such licenses.
    5. To protect the general public against unscrupulous brokers and salesmen.
    The CORRECT combination is:

    A. 1, 3, 5   B. 1, 2, 3, 4   C. 1, 4   D. all of the above

13. Which combination of the following statements is TRUE?
    1. Everyone engaged in the business of real property management requires a license as a broker or salesman.
    2. One act as a real estate broker or salesman will require a person engaged in such business to take out a license.
    3. An applicant for a broker's license is not required to file a bond.
    4. An applicant for a real estate license may not engage in the real estate business until the license is in his possession or in the possession of the broker and has been registered with the clerk of the court.
    The CORRECT combination is:

    A. 1, 2   B. 3 only   C. 1, 4   D. 1, 2, 4

14. The purpose of posting a bond in connection with the application for a real estate broker's license is
    1. to ensure the faithful observance of all the provisions of the law
    2. to make it difficult for the financially insecure to become real estate brokers
    3. that the bond shall indemnify any person who may be damaged by a failure on the part of an applicant for a real estate license to conduct his business in accordance with the requirements of the license law
    4. to give the government another source of revenue

15. Which combination of the following statements is FALSE?
    1. Before a client signs a purchase agreement, the broker or salesman has a positive duty to explain the agreement in detail.
    2. Upon receipt of the licenses by the broker, he must register them with the clerk of courts or display them in his place of business.
    3. Immediately upon the termination of the association of a real estate salesman with his broker, the broker shall return the salesman's license to the real estate commission for cancellation.
    4. In case of any change of business location, the broker must notify the real estate commission and return his license to the commission, whereupon a new license will be issued.
    The CORRECT combination is:

    A. 1, 2   B. 3, 4   C. 2 only   D. 1, 2, 4

16. Which of the following activities are NOT lawfully allowed to be performed by a licensed real estate salesman?
    1. Transact any real estate brokerage business in his own name
    2. Open and maintain a branch office in his own name
    3. Employ salesmen
    4. Advertise and list, using his own name
    5. Close deals
    The CORRECT combination is:

    A. all of the above   B. 1, 4   C. 5 only   D. 3, 4, 5

17. Which combination of the following statements is TRUE?
    1. If a real estate license is not registered with the clerk of courts, it is invalid.
    2. A real estate broker is liable for frauds and misrepresentations of any salesman associated with him, even where the broker has no knowledge of the misrepresentation.
    3. A real estate salesman may receive compensation from any broker with whom he has dealings.
    4. The salesman must keep his license in his personal possession.
    The CORRECT combination is:

    A. 1 only   B. 1, 2   C. 1, 2, 3   D. 4 only

18. Which combination of the following statements is FALSE?
    1. It is unnecessary to register your license.
    2. You must be an American citizen to obtain a broker's or salesman's license.
    3. The division of commission between a broker and his salesman is determined by their agreement.
    4. A salesman may engage in the real estate business before his license is received from the commission.
    The CORRECT combination is:

    A. 1, 2   B. 2, 3   C. 1, 4   D. 1, 2, 4

19. Which combination of the following statements is FALSE?
    1. Attorneys are exempt from the real estate license law requirements.
    2. A person who gives only part of his time to the real estate business has to secure a license.
    3. An agreement of sale is simply one's consent that he intends to sell; a deed is evidence that he has bought and is now the owner of the property.
    4. The terms "real estate broker" and "Realtor" mean the same thing.
    The CORRECT combination is:

    A. 1, 2   B. 1, 2, 4   C. 1 only   D. 4 only

20. Which of the following are duties owed by a real estate broker to his client?
    1. To act for his client as he would if the property were his own.
    2. To treat fairly and without bias the person on the other side of the transaction.
    3. To offer property solely on its merit without exaggeration, concealment, or misrepresentation.
    4. To protect the public against fraud or unethical practices.
    The CORRECT combination is:

    A. 2, 3   B. 2 only   C. 2, 3, 4   D. all of the above

21. Which combination of the following statements is *FALSE*?
    1. A real estate broker may never receive compensation from both parties to a sale or trade.
    2. The terms "realty," "real estate," and "real property" are interchangeable.
    3. A deed conveying property to a creditor as security for the payment of a debt is called a mortgage.
    4. The code of ethics governs the conduct of licensed brokers and salesmen.
    The *CORRECT* combination is:

    A. 1 only
    B. 1,4
    C. 1,2
    D. none of the above

22. Which statements concerning the deposit are *TRUE*?
    1. The broker and the salesman may split the deposit according to their agreement.
    2. The deposit is part of the purchase price paid by the buyer.
    3. Neither the broker nor the salesman has the right to the deposit.
    4. The seller pays for the services of the broker -- the buyer's deposit is to the seller.
    The *CORRECT* statements are:

    A. 1, 2, 4   B. 1, 4   C. 2, 3   D. 2, 3, 4

23. Which combination of the following statements is *TRUE*?
    1. If a salesman is personally convinced that a certain piece of property will increase in value, he can lawfully guarantee a future profit to the prospective purchaser.
    2. A real estate broker is one employed for negotiating the sale, purchase, or exchange of real estate for a commission contingent on success.
    3. A real estate salesman is one employed by a broker to procure a sale, purchase, or exchange of real estate.
    4. The holding of a salesman's license authorizes the licensee to list or advertise property in his own name.
    The *CORRECT* combination is:

    A. 2, 3   B. 1, 2, 3   C. 2, 3, 4   D. 1, 2, 3, 4

24. A real estate salesman is paid by the

    A. seller
    B. buyer
    C. broker to whom his license is issued
    D. escrow agent

25. A real estate salesman is entitled to receive

    A. 1/2 of the 5% commission
    B. what the broker decides is fair
    C. what he has earned, according to his agreement with the broker
    D. none of the above

KEY (CORRECT ANSWERS)

1.	B	11.	B
2.	B	12.	D
3.	A	13.	D
4.	B	14.	A
5.	D	15.	C
6.	A	16.	A
7.	B	17.	B
8.	C	18.	C
9.	B	19.	D
10.	D	20.	D

21. A
22. D
23. A
24. C
25. C

TEST 6

DIRECTIONS: Each question or incomplete statement is followed by several suggested answers or completions. Select the one that *BEST* answers the question or completes the statement. *PRINT THE LETTER OF THE CORRECT ANSWER IN THE SPACE AT THE RIGHT.*

1. Every real estate license *MUST* be registered at the   1.____

    A. office of the real estate commission
    B. local real estate board
    C. county clerk's office
    D. recorder's office

2. The license of a real estate broker or salesman may be revoked or suspended for violation of the real estate license law by   2.____

    A. the division of licenses and permits
    B. the court
    C. the National Association of real estate boards
    D. the state real estate commission

3. A licensed real estate salesman is permitted by law to represent   3.____

    A. several brokers
    B. only his employing broker
    C. himself as broker
    D. an interested third party

4. When a salesman is discharged or leaves the employ of a broker, the broker should   4.____

    A. give the salesman his license
    B. notify the local real estate board
    C. inform the salesman by telephone
    D. send the salesman's license to the real estate commission for cancellation, informing the salesman by letter, and sending a copy to the commission

5. To operate a branch office a broker *MUST*   5.____

    A. find a good location
    B. have his license endorsed to cover the branch office
    C. obtain a branch office license from the state real estate commission
    D. have 10 years' experience

6. A real estate salesman, upon receiving a deposit, should   6.____

    A. turn it over to the seller, less commission
    B. use it to cover expenses of the transaction
    C. give it to the broker to be placed in an escrow account
    D. give a party for the office staff

7. A copy of a broker's bond should be   7.____

    A. kept in a bank box
    B. displayed in the broker's office in public view
    C. kept in the office safe
    D. carried on the broker's person

8. Upon being sued in a real estate transaction, a salesman or broker should

   A. notify the state real estate commission
   B. leave the state
   C. effect a compromise
   D. declare bankruptcy

9. A salesman's license stays in the possession of

   A. the salesman
   B. the commission
   C. his broker
   D. his next of kin

10. Anyone operating in the real estate brokerage business without a license

    A. is subject to a fine and imprisonment
    B. is considered unethical
    C. is barred from ever getting a license
    D. cannot hire licensed salesmen

11. A broker should furnish a bond

    A. in an amount set by his state
    B. in his county of residence
    C. after he has been sued
    D. if he is insolvent

12. When a broker and salesman have a dispute over the commission, they should

    A. discuss it with buyer and seller
    B. each consult an attorney
    C. contact the real estate commission in writing
    D. request a hearing from the commission

13. The amount of commission to be paid a broker is fixed by

    A. statute law
    B. the department of occupational standards
    C. the state real estate commission
    D. agreement of the parties

14. To file a complaint against a licensed salesman or broker for one or more causes for revocation or suspension of a license, the complainant should

    A. telephone the state real estate commission
    B. write a letter to the department of occupational standards
    C. go to the commission to give an oral report of the details
    D. file the charges or complaint in affidavit form with the state real estate commission

15. To use the word "Realtor," a licensed broker MUST

    A. pass a written examination
    B. be issued a real estate license
    C. be an active member of a local real estate board
    D. be a member of the state commission

16. Unlicensed persons *CANNOT* legally collect a brokerage fee or commission because it is   16.____

    A. unethical
    B. against the rules of the local board
    C. not in the contract
    D. illegal

17. A corporation may engage in the real estate brokerage business only when the officer acting for the corporation   17.____

    A. is a duly licensed salesman
    B. has authority from the corporation commissioner
    C. is a licensed broker
    D. is the president of the corporation

18. The real estate law provides that all applicants for a real estate salesman's license MUST be   18.____

    A. a resident of the state for at least one year
    B. at least 21 years of age
    C. a citizen of the United States
    D. none of the above

19. Real property security dealers, who are required to file and maintain with the real estate commissioner a bond issued by an admitted corporate surety insurer, would have to file such a bond in the amount of   19.____

    A. $5,000   B. $7,500   C. $10,000   D. none of the above

20. A person who is engaged *SOLELY* in the appraisal of real estate is required to hold   20.____

    A. a real estate broker's license
    B. a real estate appraiser's license
    C. a membership card as a M.A.I.
    D. none of the above

21. Which of the following activities require a license in order to be performed by one on behalf of another for a stated compensation?   21.____
    1. To lease a summer house
    2. To offer to sell a bakery business
    3. To offer to exchange lands
    4. To appraise a going concern
    The *CORRECT* combination is:

    A. 1, 3   B. 1 only   C. 1, 4   D. all of the above

22. The term "compensation" includes   22.____

    A. salary   B. a fee
    C. commission   D. all of the above

23. The term "valuable consideration" includes

    A. only money consideration
    B. the granting of a favor
    C. anything of value
    D. all of the above

24. The term "real estate" refers to

    A. the land and all the buildings, fixtures, and improvements attached thereto
    B. the land only
    C. only buildings
    D. the land and all buildings only

25. Which of the following are "persons" within the meaning of the real estate law?
    1. Individuals
    2. Firms
    3. Co-partnerships
    4. Associations
    5. Corporations

    The CORRECT combination is:

    A. 1 only   B. 1, 5   C. 2, 5   D. 1, 2, 3, 4, 5

KEY (CORRECT ANSWERS)

1. C	11. A
2. D	12. B
3. B	13. D
4. D	14. D
5. C	15. C
6. C	16. D
7. B	17. C
8. A	18. D
9. C	19. D
10. A	20. D

21. D
22. D
23. D
24. A
25. D

EXAMINATION SECTION
TEST 1

DIRECTIONS: Each question or incomplete statement is followed by several suggested answers or completions. Select the one that BEST answers the question or completes the statement. *PRINT THE LETTER OF THE CORRECT ANSWER IN THE SPACE AT THE RIGHT.*

1. $600 is 12 1/2% of what amount?

    A. $3,600   B. $4,000   C. $4,480   D. $4,800   E. $5,000

2. A lot is 125 feet wide and 165 feet deep. It sells for $13,750. What was the price per front foot?

    A. $50   B. $70   C. $90   D. $110   E. $130

3. Ronald Munson, salesman, is working on a 50-50 split commission basis with his employing broker, Bart Dodge. Munson sells a 280-acre farm for $165 per acre. The commission schedule for the Dodge Agency calls for 5% on the first $20,000; 3 1/2% on the next $10,000; and 2 1/2% on the balance. What is Munson's commission?

    A. $622.30   B. $688.88   C. $701.23   D. $825.00   E. $877.50

4. The real value of a certain property is $8,500.00. It is assessed at 33 1/3% of its real value. It is taxed at the rate of $2.45 per $100 on the assessed value. What are the taxes?

    A. $52.30   B. $61.70   C. $69.41   D. $75.00   E. $80.25

5. A farm of sixty acres listed for sale at $150 per acre was sold for $7,650 on condition that the purchaser pay the 10% sales commission charged of the selling price. How much money did the buyer actually save on the transaction?

    A. $490.00   B. $525.00   C. $548.80   D. $575.00   E. $585.00

6. If 4% was the interest rate and the quarterly interest payment on a loan amounted to $117.25, the amount of the principal would be

    A. $10,000   B. $11,725   C. $12,100   D. $12,500   E. $13,300

7. What is the amount of interest on a loan of $10,000 at 6% per year for four months?

    A. $50   B. $100   C. $150   D. $200   E. $250

8. What will the taxes be for six months on property valued at $8,000 if the tax rate is $2.27 per $100 valuation per year?

    A. $75.00   B. $80.40   C. $90.80   D. $95.00   E. $98.40

9. What is the purchase price when a 20% downpayment is $2,500?

    A. $11,000   B. $11,500   C. $12,000   D. $12,500   E. $13,000

10. An acre of land contains 43,560 sq.ft. What is the cost of a lot 132 feet by 330 feet deep at $800.00 per acre?

    A. $500   B. $600   C. $700   D. $800   E. $900

KEY (CORRECT ANSWERS)

1. D   6. B
2. D   7. D
3. E   8. C
4. C   9. D
5. E   10. D

TEST 2

DIRECTIONS: Each question or incomplete statement is followed by several suggested answers or completions. Select the one that BEST answers the question or completes the statement. PRINT THE LETTER OF THE CORRECT ANSWER IN THE SPACE AT THE RIGHT.

1. A section of land contains 640 acres, At $100 per acre, what is the cost of a quarter section? 1.____

   A. $12,000   B. $14,000   C. $16,000   D. $18,000   E. $20,000

2. At $75 per front foot, what is the cost of a lot 80 feet front by 120 feet deep? 2.____

   A. $1,000   B. $3,000   C. $4,000   D. $5,000   E. $6,000

3. What is the salesman's share when he is entitled to one-half of a 5% commission on a $15,000 sale? 3.____

   A. $125   B. $250   C. $375   D. $500   E. $625

4. A house rented for $135 per month. What is the rent for 23 days (based on a 30-day month)? 4.____

   A. $87.50   B. $91.30   C. $97.75   D. $102.90   E. $103.50

5. Two real estate salesmen employed by two different brokers cooperate in selling a property for $35,000. A 5% commission was paid by the owner. Each salesman received 60% of all commissions he earned for the broker. Both brokers agreed to divide the earned commission equally. How much commission did each salesman receive? 5.____

   A. $125   B. $225   C. $325   D. $425   E. $525

6. A store averages $600 per month rent on a percentage lease of 6% on gross sales. What are the gross sales? 6.____

   A. $80,000   B. $90,000   C. $100,000
   D. $110,000   E. $120,000

7. A motel has 24 units. The average rental is $5.00 per unit for a thirty-day month. The vacancy factor is 16%. What is the income per month? 7.____

   A. $2,872   B. $3,024   C. $3,192
   D. $3,876   E. $4,002.20

8. A man built a house which was rectangular in shape. The dimensions were 24 feet wide by 36 feet long by 14 feet high. What is the total number of square feet in this house? 8.____

   A. 664   B. 728   C. 788   D. 864   E. 912

9. John Doe built a house which was 28 feet wide by 42 feet long. It was a ranch-type house. The cost of building averaged $14.75 per square foot. What was the cost of the house? 9.____

   A. $15,266.36   B. $16,777.00   C. $17,346.00
   D. $18,294.00   E. $19,336.00

10. What is three-months' interest on $566.66 at 5% per annum? 10.___
    A. $3.08   B. $4.08   C. $5.08   D. $6.08   E. $7.08

KEY (CORRECT ANSWERS)

1. C
2. E
3. C
4. E
5. E

6. E
7. B
8. D
9. C
10. E

GLOSSARY OF REAL ESTATE TERMS

CONTENTS

	Page
Abstract of Title................Appraisal by Summation	1
Appurtenance.......................Cancellation Clause	2
Caveat Emptor...............................Conveyance	3
County Clerk's Certificate.... Documentary Evidence	4
Duress....................................Exclusive Agency	5
Exclusive Right to Sell......................Ground Rent	6
Habendum Clause................................ Landlord	7
Lease..Mortgagee	8
Mortgagor...Party Wall	9
Percentage Lease..................................Release	10
Release Clause....................Subordination Clause	11
Subscribing Witness..............................Valuation	12
Vendee's Lien..... ....Zoning Ordinance	13

GLOSSARY OF REAL ESTATE TERMS

A

Abstract of Title—A summary of all of the recorded instruments and proceedings which affect the title to property, arranged in chronological order.

Accretion—The addition to land through processes of nature, as by streams or wind.

Accrued Interest—Accrue: to grow; to be added to. Accrued interest is interest that has been earned but not due and payable.

Acknowledgment—A formal declaration before a duly authorized officer by a person who has executed an instrument that such execution is the person's act and deed.

Acquisition—An act or process by which a person procures property.

Acre—A measure of land equaling 160 square rods or 4,840 square yards or 43,560 feet.

Adjacent—Lying near to but not necessarily in actual contact with.

Adjoining—Contiguous; attaching, in actual contact with.

Administrator—A person appointed by court to administer the estate of a deceased person who left no will; i.e., who died intestate.

Ad Valorem—According to valuation.

Adverse Possession—A means of acquiring title where an occupant has been in actual, open, notorious, exclusive, and continuous occupancy of property under a claim of right for the required statutory period.

Affidavit—A statement or declaration reduced to writing, and sworn to or affirmed before some officer who is authorized to administer an oath or affirmation.

Affirm—To confirm, to ratify, to verify.

Agency—That relationship between principal and agent which arises out of a contract either expressed or implied, written or oral, wherein an agent is employed by a person to do certain acts on the person's behalf in dealing with a third party.

Agent—One who undertakes to transact some business or to manage some affair for another by authority of the latter.

Agreement of Sale—A written agreement between seller and purchaser in which the purchaser agrees to buy certain real estate and the seller agrees to sell upon terms and conditions set forth therein.

Alienation—A transferring of property to another; the transfer of property and possession of lands, or other things, from one person to another

Amortization—A gradual paying off of a debt by periodical installments.

Apportionments—Adjustment of the income, expenses or carrying charges of real estate usually computed to the date of closing of title so that the seller pays all expenses to that date. The buyer assumes all expenses commencing the date the deed is conveyed to the buyer.

Appraisal—An estimate of a property's valuation by an appraiser who is usually presumed to be expert in this work.

Appraisal by Capitalization—An estimate of value by capitalization of productivity and income.

Appraisal by Comparison—Comparability with the sale prices of other similar properties.

Appraisal by Summation—Adding together all parts of a property separately appraised to form a whole: e.g., value of the land considered as vacant added to the cost of reproduction of the building, less depreciation.

Appurtenance—Something which is outside the property itself but belongs to the land and adds to its greater enjoyment such as a right of way or a barn or a dwelling.

Assessed Valuation—A valuation placed upon property by a public officer or a board, as a basis for taxation.

Assessment—A charge against real estate made by a unit of government to cover a proportionate cost of an improvement such as a street or sewer.

Assessor—An official who has the responsibility of determining assessed values.

Assignee—The person to whom an agreement or contract is assigned.

Assignment—The method or manner by which a right, a specialty, or contract is transferred from one person to another.

Assignor—A party who assigns or transfers an agreement or contract to another.

Assumption of Mortgage—The taking of title to property by a grantee, wherein the grantee assumes liability for payment of an existing note or bond secured by a mortgage against a property and becomes personally liable for the payment of such mortgage debt.

Attest—To witness to; to witness by observation and signature.

Avulsion—The removal of land from one owner to another, when a stream suddenly changes its channel.

B

Beneficiary—The person who receives or is to receive the benefits resulting from certain acts.

Bequeath—To give or hand down by will; to leave by will.

Bequest—That which is given by the terms of a will.

Bill of Sale—A written instrument given to pass title of personal property from vendor to vendee.

Binder—An agreement to cover the down payment for the purchase of real estate as evidence of good faith on the part of the purchaser.

Blanket Mortgage—A single mortgage which covers more than one piece of real estate.

Bona Fide—In good faith, without fraud.

Bond—The evidence of a personal debt which is secured by a mortgage or other lien on real estate.

Building Codes—Regulations established by local governments stating fully the structural requirements for building.

Building Line—A line fixed at a certain distance from the front and/or sides of a lot, beyond which no building can project.

Building Loan Agreement—An agreement whereby the lender advances money to an owner with provisional payments at certain stages of construction.

C

Cancellation Clause—A provision in a lease which confers upon one or more or all of the parties to the lease the right to terminate the party's or parties' obligations thereunder upon the occurrence of the condition or contingency set forth in the said clause.

Caveat Emptor—Let the buyer beware. The buyer must examine the goods or property and buy at the buyer's own risk.

Cease and Desist Order—An order executed by the Secretary of State directing broker recipients to cease and desist from all solicitation of homeowners whose names and addresses appear on the list(s) forwarded with such order. The order acknowledges petition filings by homeowners listed evidencing their premises are not for sale, thereby revoking the implied invitation to solicit. The issuance of a Cease and Desist Order does not prevent an owner from selling or listing his premises for sale. It prohibits soliciting by licensees served with such order and subjects violators to penalties of suspension or revocation of their licenses as provided in section 441-c of the Real Property Law.

Cease and Desist Petition—A statement filed by a homeowner showing address of premises owned which notifies the Department of State that such premises are not for sale and does not wish to be solicited. In so doing, petitioner revokes the implied invitation to be solicited, by any means with respect thereto, by licensed real estate brokers and salespersons.

Certiorari—A proceeding to review in a competent court the action of an inferior tribunal board or officer exercising judicial functions.

Chain of Title—A history of conveyances and encumbrances affecting a title from the time the original patent was granted, or as far back as records are available.

Chattel—Personal property, such as household goods or fixtures.

Chattel Mortgage—A mortgage on personal property.

Client—The one by whom a broker is employed and by whom the broker will be compensated on completion of the purpose of the agency.

Closing Date—The date upon which the buyer takes over the property; usually between 30 and 60 days after the signing of the contract. Cloud on the Title An outstanding claim or encumbrance which, if valid, would affect or impair the owner's title.

Collateral—Additional security pledged for the payment of an obligation.

Color of Title—That which appears to be good title, but which is not title in fact.

Commission—A sum due a real estate broker for services in that capacity.

Commitment—A pledge or a promise or affirmation agreement.

Condemnation—Taking private property for public use, with fair compensation to the owner; exercising the right of eminent domain.

Conditional Sales Contract—A contract for the sale of property stating that delivery is to be made to the buyer, title to remain vested in the seller until the conditions of the contract have been fulfilled.

Consideration—Anything of value given to induce entering into a contract; it may be money, personal services, or even love and affection.

Constructive Notice—Information or knowledge of a fact imputed by law to a person because the person could have discovered the fact by proper diligence and inquiry; (public records).

Contract—An agreement between competent parties to do or not to do certain things for a legal consideration, whereby each party acquires a right to what the other possesses.

Conversion—Change from one character or use to another.

Conveyance—The transfer of the title of land from one to another. The means or medium by which title of real estate is transferred.

County Clerk's Certificate—When an acknowledgment is taken by an officer not authorized in the state or county where the document is to be recorded, the instrument which must be attached to the acknowledgment is called a county clerk's certificate. It is given by the clerk of the county where the officer obtained his/her authority and certifies to the officer's signature and powers.

Covenants—Agreements written into deeds and other instruments promising performance or nonperformance of certain acts, or stipulating certain uses or nonuse's of the property.

D

Damages—The indemnity recoverable by a person who has sustained an injury, either to his/her person, property or relative rights, through the act or default of another.

Decedent—One who is dead.

Decree Order issued by one in authority; an edict or law; a judicial decision.

Dedication—A grant and appropriation of land by its owner for some public use, accepted for such use, by an authorized public official on behalf of the public.

Deed—An instrument in writing duly executed and delivered, that conveys title to real property.

Deed Restriction—An imposed restriction in a deed for the purpose of limiting the use of the land such as: A restriction against the sale of liquor thereon. A restriction As to the size, type, value or placement of improvements that may be erected thereon.

Default—Failure to fulfill a duty or promise, or to discharge an obligation; omission or failure to perform any acts.

Defendant—The party sued or called to answer in any suit, civil or criminal, at law or in equity.

Deficiency Judgment—A judgment given when the security for a loan does not entirely satisfy the debt upon its default.

Delivery—The transfer of the possession of a thing from one person to another.

Demising Clause—A clause found in a lease whereby the landlord (lessor) leases and the tenant (lessee) takes the property.

Depreciation—Loss of value in real property brought about by age, physical deterioration, or functional or economic obsolescence.

Descent—When an owner of real estate dies intestate, the owner's property descends, by operation of law, to the owner's distributees.

Devise—A gift of real estate by will or last testament.

Devisee—One who receives a bequest of real estate made by will.

Devisor—One who bequeaths real estate by will.

Directional Growth—The location or direction toward which the residential sections of a city are destined or determined to grow.

Dispossess Proceedings—Summary process by a landlord to oust a tenant and regain possession of the premises for nonpayment of rent or other breach of conditions of the lease or occupancy.

Distributee—Person receiving or entitled to receive land as representative of the former owner.

Documentary Evidence—Evidence in the form of written or printed papers.

Duress—Unlawful constraint exercised upon a person whereby the person is forced to do some act against his will.

Earnest Money—Down payment made by a purchaser of real estate as evidence of good faith.

Easement—A right that may be exercised by the public or individuals on, over or through the lands of others.

Ejectment—A form of action to regain possession of real property, with damages for the unlawful retention; used when there is no relationship of landlord and tenant.

Eminent Domain—A right of the government to acquire property for necessary public use by condemnation; the owner must be fairly compensated.

Encroachment—A building, part of a building, or obstruction which intrudes upon or invades a highway or sidewalk or trespasses upon the property of another.

Encumbrance—Any right to or interest in land that diminishes its value. (Also Incumbrance)

Endorsement—An act of signing one's name on the back of a check or note, with or without further qualifications.

Equity—The interest or value which the owner has in real estate over and above the liens against it.

Equity of Redemption—A right of the owner to reclaim property before it is sold through foreclosure proceedings, by the payment of the debt, interest and costs.

Erosion—The wearing away of land through processes of nature, as by streams and winds.

Escheat—The reversion to the state of property in event the owner thereof dies, without leaving a will and has no distributees to whom the property may pass by lawful descent.

Escrow—A written agreement between two or more parties providing that certain instruments or property be placed with a third party to be delivered to a designated person upon the fulfillment or performance of some act or condition.

Estate—The degree, quantity, nature and extent of interest which a person has in real property.

Estate for Life—An estate or interest held during the terms of some certain person's life.

Estate in Reversion—The residue of an estate left for the grantor, to commence in possession after the termination of some particular estate granted by the grantor.

Estate at Will—The occupation of lands and tenements by a tenant for an indefinite period, terminable by one or both parties at will.

Estoppel Certificate—An instrument executed by the mortgagor setting forth the present status and the balance due on the mortgage as of the date of the execution of the certificate. A legal proceeding by a lessor landlord to recover possession of real property.

Eviction, Actual—Where one is, either by force or by process of law, actually put out of possession.

Eviction, Constructive—Any disturbance of the tenant's possessions by the landlord whereby the premises are rendered unfit or unsuitable for the purpose for which they were leased.

Eviction, Partial—Where the possessor of the premises is deprived of a portion thereof.

Exclusive Agency—An agreement of employment of a broker to the exclusion of all other brokers; if sale is made by any other broker during term of employment, broker holding exclusive agency is entitled to commissions in addition to the commissions payable to the broker who effected the transaction.

Exclusive Right to Sell—An agreement of employment by a broker under which the exclusive right to sell for a specified period is granted to the broker; if a sale during the term of the agreement is made by the owner or by any other broker, the broker holding such exclusive right to sell is nevertheless entitled to compensation.

Executor—A male person or a corporate entity or any other type of organization named or designated in a will to carry out its provisions as to the disposition of the estate of a deceased person.

Executrix—A woman appointed to perform the duties similar to those of an executor.

Extension Agreement—An agreement which extends the life of the mortgage to a later date.

F

Fee; Fee Simple; Fee Absolute—Absolute ownership of real property; a person has this type of estate where the person is entitled to the entire property with unconditional power of disposition during the person's life and descending to the person's distributees and legal representatives upon the person's death intestate.

Fiduciary—A person who on behalf of or for the benefit of another transacts business or handles money on property not the person's own; such relationship implies great confidence and trust.

Fixtures—Personal property so attached to the land or improvements as to become part of the real property.

Foreclosure—A procedure whereby property pledged as security for a debt is sold to pay the debt in the event of default in payments or terms.

Forfeiture—Loss of money or anything of value, by way of penalty due to failure to perform.

Freehold—An interest in real estate, not less than an estate for life. (Use of this term discontinued Sept. 1, 1967.)

Front Foot—A standard measurement, one foot wide, of the width of land, applied at the frontage on its street line. Each front foot extends the depth of the lot.

G

Grace Period—Additional time allowed to perform an act or make a payment before a default occurs.

Graduated Leases—A lease which provides for a graduated change at stated intervals in the amount of the rent to be paid; used largely in long term leases.

Grant—A technical term used in deeds of conveyance of lands to indicate a transfer. Grantee The party to whom the title to real property is conveyed.

Grantor—The person who conveys real estate by deed; the seller.

Gross Income—Total income from property before any expenses are deducted.

Gross Lease—A lease of property whereby the lessor is to meet all property charges regularly incurred through ownership.

Ground Rent—Earnings of improved property credited to earning of the ground itself after allowance made for earnings of improvements.

H

Habendum Clause—The "To Have and To Hold" clause which defines or limits the quantity of the estate granted in the premises of the deed.

Hereditaments—The largest classification of property; including lands, tenements and incorporeal property, such as rights of way.

Holdover Tenant—A tenant who remains in possession of leased property after the expiration of the lease term.

Hypothecate—To give a thing as security without the necessity of giving up possession of it.

I

In Rem—A proceeding against the realty directly; as distinguished from a proceeding against a person. (Used in taking land for nonpayment of taxes, etc.)

Incompetent—A person who is unable to manage his/her own affairs by reason of insanity, inbecility or feeble-mindedness.

Incumbrance—Any right to or interest in land that diminishes its value. (Also Encumbrance)

Injunction—A writ or order issued under the seal of a court to restrain one or more parties to a suit or proceeding from doing an act which is deemed to be inequitable or unjust in regard to the rights of some other party or parties in the suit or proceeding.

Installments—Parts of the same debt, payable at successive periods as agreed; payments made to reduce a mortgage.

Instrument—A written legal document; created to effect the rights of the parties. Interest

Rate—The percentage of a sum of money charged for its use.

Intestate—A person who dies having made no will, or leaves one which is defective in form, in which case the person's estate descends to the person's distributees.

Involuntary Lien—A lien imposed against property without consent of the owner, i.e., taxes, special assessments.

Irrevocable—Incapable of being recalled or revoked; unchangeable; unalterable.

J

Jeopardy—Peril, danger.

Joint Tenancy—Ownership of realty by two or more persons, each of whom has an undivided interest with the "right of survivorship."

Judgment—Decree of a court declaring that one individual is indebted to another, and fixing the amount of such indebtedness.

Junior Mortgage—A mortgage second in lien to a previous mortgage.

L

Laches—Delay or negligence in asserting one's legal rights.

Land, Tenements and Hereditaments—A phrase used in the early English Law, to express all sorts of property of the immovable class.

Landlord—One who rents property to another.

Lease—A contract whereby, for a consideration, usually termed rent, one who is entitled to the possession of real property transfers such rights to another for life, for a term of years, or at will. Leasehold The interest or estate which a lessee of real estate has therein by virtue of the lessee's lease.

Lessee—A person to whom property is rented under a lease.

Lessor—One who rents property to another under a lease.

Lien—A legal right or claim upon a specific property which attaches to the property until a debt is satisfied.

Lien (Mechanic's)—A notice filed with the County Clerk stating that payment has not been made for an improvement to real property. Life Estate The conveyance of title to property for the duration of the life of the grantee.

Life Tenant—The holder of a life estate.

Lis Pendens—A legal document, filed in the office of the county clerk giving notice that an action or proceeding is pending in the courts affecting the title to the property.

Listing—An employment contract between principal and agent, authorizing the agent to perform services for the principal involving the latter's property.

Litigation—The act of carrying on a lawsuit.

M

Mandatory—Requiring strict conformity or obedience.

Market Value—The highest price which a buyer, willing but not compelled to buy, would pay, and the lowest a seller, willing but not compelled to sell, would accept.

Marketable Title—A title which a court of equity considers to be so free from defect that it will enforce its acceptance by a purchaser.

Mechanic's Lien—A lien given by law upon a building or other improvement upon land, and upon the land itself, to secure the price of labor done upon, and materials furnished for, the improvement.

Meeting of the Minds—Whenever all parties to a contract agree to the exact terms thereof.

Metes and Bounds—A term used in describing the boundary lines of land, setting forth all the boundary lines together with their terminal points and angles.

Minor—A person under an age specified by law; under 18 years of age.

Monument—A fixed object and point established by surveyors to establish land locations.

Moratorium—An emergency act by a legislative body to suspend the legal enforcement of contractual obligations.

Mortgage—An instrument in writing, duly executed and delivered, that creates a lien upon real estate as security for the payment of a specified debt, which is usually in the form of a bond.

Mortgage Commitment—A formal indication, by a lending institution that it will grant a mortgage loan on property, in a certain specified amount and on certain specified terms. Mortgage Reduction Certificate An instrument executed by the mortgagee, setting forth the present status and the balance due on the mortgage as of the date of the execution of the instrument.

Mortgagee—The party who lends money and takes a mortgage to secure the payment thereof.

Mortgagor—A person who borrows money and gives a mortgage on the person's property as security for the payment of the debt.

Multiple Listing—An arrangement among Real Estate Board of Exchange Members, whereby each broker presents the broker's listings to the attention of the other members so that if a sale results, the commission is divided between the broker bringing the listing and the broker making the sale.

N

Net Listing—A price below which an owner will not sell the property, and at which price a broker will not receive a commission; the broker receives the excess over and above the net listing as the broker's commission.

Notary Public—A public officer who is authorized to take acknowledgments to certain classes of documents, such as deeds, contracts, mortgages, and before whom affidavits may be sworn.

O

Obligee—The person in whose favor an obligation is entered into.

Obligor—The person who binds himself/herself to another; one who has engaged to perform some obligation; one who makes a bond.

Obsolescence—Loss in value due to reduced desirability and usefulness of a structure because its design and construction become obsolete; loss because of becoming old-fashioned, and not in keeping with modern means, with consequent loss of income.

Open End Mortgage—A mortgage under which the mortgagor may secure additional funds from the mortgagee, usually up to but not exceeding the original amount of the existing amortizing mortgage.

Open Listing—A listing given to any number of brokers without liability to compensate any except the one who first secures a buyer ready, willing and able to meet the terms of the listing, or secures the acceptance by the seller of a satisfactory offer; the sale of the property automatically terminates the listing.

Open Mortgage—A mortgage that has matured or is overdue and, therefore, is "open" to foreclosure at any time.

Option—A right given for a consideration to purchase or lease a property upon specified terms within a specified time; if the right is not exercised the option holder is not subject to liability for damages; if exercised, the grantor of option must perform.

P

Partition—The division which is made of real property between those who own it in undivided shares.

Party Wall—A party wall is a wall built along the line separating two properties, partly on each, which wall either owner, the owner's heirs and assigns has the right to use; such right constituting an easement over so much of the adjoining owner's land as is covered by the wall.

Percentage Lease—A lease of property in which the rental is based upon the percentage of the volume of sales made upon the leased premises, usually provides for minimum rental.

Personal Property—Any property which is not real property.

Plat Book—A public record containing maps of land showing the division of such land into streets, blocks and lots and indicating the measurements of the individual parcels.

Plottage—Increment in unity value of a plot of land created by assembling smaller ownerships into one ownership.

Police Power—The right of any political body to enact laws and enforce them, for the order, safety, health, morals and general welfare of the public.

Power of Attorney—A written instrument duly signed and executed by an owner of property, which authorizes an agent to act on behalf of the owner to the extent indicated in the instrument.

Premises—Lands and tenements; an estate; the subject matter of a conveyance.

Prepayment Clause—A clause in a mortgage which gives a mortgagor the privilege of paying the mortgage indebtedness before it becomes due.

Principal—The employer of an agent or broker; the broker's or agent's client.

Probate—To establish the will of a deceased person.

Purchase Money Mortgage—A mortgage given by a grantee in part payment of the purchase price of real estate.

Q

Quiet Enjoyment—The right of an owner or a person legally in possession to the use of property without interference of possession.

Quiet Title Suit—A suit in court to remove a defect, cloud or suspicion regarding legal rights of an owner to a certain parcel of real property.

Quitclaim Deed—A deed which conveys simply the grantor's rights or interest in real estate, without any agreement or covenant as to the nature or extent of that interest, or any other covenants; usually used to remove a cloud from the title.

R

Real Estate Board—An organization whose members consist primarily of real estate brokers and salespersons.

Real Property—Land, and generally whatever is erected upon or affixed thereto.

Realtor—A coined word which may only be used by an active member of a local real estate board, affiliated with the National Association of Real Estate Boards.

Recording—The act of writing or entering in a book of public record instruments affecting the title to real property.

Redemption—The right of a mortgagor to redeem the property by paying a debt after the expiration date and before sale at foreclosure; the right of an owner to reclaim the owner's property after the sale for taxes.

Release—The act or writing by which some claim or interest is surrendered to another.

Release Clause—A clause found in a blanket mortgage which gives the owner of the property the privilege of paying off a portion of the mortgage indebtedness, and thus freeing a portion of the property from the mortgage.

Rem—(See In Rem)

Remainder—An estate which takes effect after the termination of a prior estate such as a life estate.

Remainderman—The person who is to receive the property after the death of a life tenant.

Rent—The compensation paid for the use of real estate.

Reproduction Cost—Normal cost of exact duplication of a property as of a certain date.

Restriction—A limitation placed upon the use of property contained in the deed or other written instrument in the chain of title. Reversionary Interest The interest which a person has in lands or other property upon the termination of the preceding estate.

Revocation—An act of recalling a power of authority conferred, as the revocation of a power of attorney, a license, an agency, etc.

Right of Survivorship—Right of the surviving joint owner to succeed to the interests of the deceased joint owner, distinguishing feature of a joint tenancy or tenancy by the entirety.

Right of Way—The right to pass over another's land more or less frequently according to the nature of the easement.

Riparian Owner—One who owns land bounding upon a river or watercourse.

Riparian Rights—The right of a landowner to water on, under or adjacent to his land.

S

Sales Contract—A contract by which the buyer and seller agree to terms of sale.

Satisfaction Piece—An instrument for recording and acknowledging payment of an indebtedness secured by a mortgage.

Seizin—The possession of land by one who claims to own at least an estate for life therein.

Set Back—The distance from the curb or other established line, within which no buildings may be erected.

Severalty—The ownership of real property by an individual, as an individual.

Special Assessment—An assessment made against a property to pay for a public improvement by which the assessed property is supposed to be especially benefited.

Specific Performance—A remedy in a court of equity compelling a defendant to carry out the terms of an agreement or contract.

Statute—A law established by an act of the Legislature.

Statute of Frauds—State law which provides that certain contracts must be in writing in order to be enforceable at law.

Stipulations—The terms within a written contract.

Straight Line Depreciation—A definite sum set aside annually from income to pay costs of replacing improvements, without reference to the interest it earns.

Subdivision—A tract of land divided into lots or plots suitable for home building purposes.

Subletting—A leasing by a tenant to another, who holds under the tenant.

Subordination Clause—A clause which permits the placing of a mortgage at a later date which takes priority over an existing mortgage.

Subscribing Witness—One who writes his/her name as witness to the execution of an instrument.

Surety—One who guarantees the performance of another; guarantor.

Surrender—The cancellation of a lease by mutual consent of the lessor and the lessee.

Surrogate's Court (Probate Court)—A court having jurisdiction over the proof of wills, the settling of estates and of citations.

Survey—The process by which a parcel of land is measured and its area ascertained; also the blueprint showing the measurements, boundaries and area.

T

Tax Sale—Sale of property after a period of nonpayment of taxes.

Tenancy in Common—An ownership of realty by two or more persons, each of whom has an undivided interest, without the "right of survivorship."

Tenancy by the Entirety—An estate which exists only between husband and wife with equal right of possession and enjoyment during their joint lives and with the "right of survivorship."

Tenancy at Will—A license to use or occupy lands and tenements at the will of the owner.

Tenant—One who is given possession of real estate for a fixed period or at will.

Tenant at Sufferance—One who comes into possession of lands by lawful title and keeps it afterwards without any title at all.

Testate—Where a person dies leaving a valid will.

Title—Evidence that owner of land is in lawful possession thereof; evidence of ownership.

Title Insurance—A policy of insurance which indemnifies the holder for any loss sustained by reason of defects in the title.

Title Search—An examination of the public records to determine the ownership and encumbrances affecting real property.

Torrens Title—System of title records provided by state law: it is a system for the registration of land titles whereby the state of the title, showing ownership and encumbrances, can be readily ascertained from an inspection of the "register of titles" without the necessity of a search of the public records.

Tort—A wrongful act, wrong, injury; violation of a legal right.

Transfer Tax—A tax charged under certain conditions on the property belonging to an estate.

U

Unearned Increment—An increase in value of real estate due to no effort on the part of the owner; often due to increase in population.

Urban Property—City property; closely settled property.

Usury—On a loan, claiming a rate of interest greater than that permitted by law.

V

Valid—Having force, or binding force; legally sufficient and authorized by law.

Valuation—Estimated worth or price. The act of valuing by appraisal.

Vendee's Lien—A lien against property under contract of sale to secure deposit paid by a purchaser.

Verification—Sworn statements before a duly qualified officer to the correctness of the contents of an instrument.

Violations—Act, deed or conditions contrary to law or permissible use of real property.

Void—To have no force or effect; that which is unenforceable.

Voidable—That which is capable of being adjudged void, but is not void unless action is taken to make it so.

W

Waiver—The renunciation, abandonment or surrender of some claim, right or privilege.

Warranty Deed—A conveyance of land in which the grantor warrants the title to the grantee.

Will—The disposition of one's property to take effect after death.

Without Recourse—Words used in endorsing a note or bill to denote that the future holder is not to look to the endorser in case of nonpayment.

Z

Zone—An area set off by the proper authorities for specific use; subject to certain restrictions or restraints.

Zoning Ordinance—Act of city or county or other authorities specifying type and use to which property may be put in specific areas.